MW01275324

OUT OF THE SHADOWS
Real Stories from Seward, Alaska

Eagles Nest
Christian Fellowship

Published in Beaverton, Oregon, by Good Catch Publishing.
www.goodcatchpublishing.com
V1.1

Printed in the United States of America

Table of Contents

DEDICATION

This book is dedicated to the ones whose lives will be forever changed from reading these stories.

ACKNOWLEDGEMENTS

I would like to thank Pastor Dana Goodwater for the hard work, prayer and faith he put into this book to make it a reality and the people of Eagle's Nest Christian Fellowship for their boldness and vulnerability in telling the stories that comprise this compilation of real-life stories.

This book would not have been published without the amazing efforts of our project manager, Peter Bell. His untiring resolve pushed this project forward and turned it into a stunning victory. Thank you for your great fortitude and diligence. I would also like to thank our invaluable proofreader, Melody Davis, for all the focus and energy she has put into perfecting our words. Lastly, I want to extend our gratitude to Adam Anaforian, our graphic artist, whose talent and vision continually astound us. We are so blessed to have you as a part of this team.

Daren Lindley
President and CEO
Good Catch Publishing

The book you are about to read
is a compilation of authentic life stories.
The facts are true, and the events are real.
These storytellers have dealt with crisis, tragedy, abuse
and neglect and have shared their most private moments,
mess-ups and hang-ups in order for others to learn and
grow from them. In order to protect the identities of those
involved in their pasts, the names and details of some
storytellers have been withheld or changed.

INTRODUCTION

Anyone who has lived in Alaska for any length of time understands the relief the soul feels when the long nights of winter fade away. December 21 becomes a marking point for the longest night. January and February's darkness is pushed away minutes every day until the mornings are filled with the light and a new season waiting to be experienced is opened up.

Out of the Shadows relates the stories of those who have stepped out into the open light from the shadows, where it is easy to hide in life's failures and pain. These stories tell the great triumph and victory of life and things that are on the horizon. These individuals have allowed themselves to go through the process of healing, restoration and reconciliation. We all have a past; we all have things we would like to hide because of actions we have taken or trauma that has been inflicted on us. We hope that if we ignore the shadows over our past, they will fade away. But these shadows will not go on their own. They must be brought into the light.

Beyond this page are stories of seven individuals who live here in this community. They are telling their stories as a testimony to the power that comes when light meets the shadows and the dawn of a new day breaks forth, bringing healing and hope for a bright future.

THE TRIUMPH OF NAPOLEON
The Story of Kenan Napoleon
Written by Eric Ayala

According to a recent report, 77 percent of sixth-through 10th-grade students are bullied. Boys are more likely than girls to display bullying behavior through physical intimidation. Case studies done by the American Justice Department of the shooting at Columbine High School and other U.S. schools have suggested that bullying was a factor in many of the incidents. Bullying by both boys and girls is harmful and can lead to depression, body image issues and low self-esteem. According to psychologist and bullying expert Evelyn Field, bullies and targets of bullies often have undeveloped assertive communication skills. Twenty-eight percent of youth who carry weapons have witnessed violence at home.

I was a faceless and discarded victim of bullying. It seems I was ripe for the picking, as if I was born for the sadistic and abusive pleasures of other kids. Often times to combat the feelings of helplessness, I imagined various ways to get back at my attackers. Sometimes I saw myself wielding a baseball bat in a bloodied frenzy and bashing their skulls to a pulp. Or pushing them into the choppy waters of the Arctic Ocean and watching them drown like the rats they were and not lifting a finger to help.

Had I ever stood up to them, it's a sure bet that the outcome of their continual persecution would have been much different; but I never fought back — they could sense my weakness. And just like a pack of ravenous dogs, they fed off my fear.

❧❧❧

Disturbingly graphic images of retaliation consumed me as I grew up with an alcoholic mother and a dispassionate and absentee father in Anchorage, Alaska.

There were six children in the family, four boys — Christian, Charles, Jordan and myself — and two girls, Joni and Kylene. Charles was given up for adoption because Mom didn't feel she had the resources to take care of all of us.

When I was born in 1991, my mother considered giving me up to an aunt and uncle in Chevak, Alaska, for the same reason — but my aunt told her, "It's God's will that you keep him." Even though my mother drank, she appeared to have an unwavering faith in God. I was told that she would often slip away to pray and read her Bible, which caused a lot more contention between her and my dad when they were together.

My mom and dad were divorced before I was born. I don't remember a lot about him in my early years except that I was told that he drank, too, and that his drinking often led to violent outbursts. He only came back more or less when he was between jobs and needed a place to stay or needed money to buy marijuana. When he was solvent again, he'd move back out. My sisters and brothers spent several months at a time going back and forth between my parents. It never bothered me that my dad acted as if he didn't want me around. Despite the fact that I looked so much like him, he denied that I was his son. He never said anything to me directly, but whenever I did visit, there wasn't any bonding going on. He'd just glare at me, as if there were truth to his unsubstantiated accusations that my mom had been unfaithful. It made me so uncomfortable that I only wanted to be at his apartment for a few hours — I don't think I could have lasted any longer than that.

Eventually he moved back to his hometown in Hooper Bay with Christian and Jordan. Joni, Kylene and I stayed with Mom in Anchorage.

ॐॐॐ

My mother liked going to church; she would take me along to Catholic Mass when I was very little. After a while she switched to an Assemblies of God congregation that she was particularly fond of. I was the only one of the children who went with her.

"Kenan, God has plans for your life," she would say.

I remember going with her to that church for a late-night service when I was 4 years old. There was a lot of cheering and clapping and yelling, and the speaker that evening was passing out candy. Maybe it was a ploy to keep me interested, but all I wanted to do was sleep.

Whenever Mom drank at home, she loved loud music. Pink Floyd, Ozzy Osbourne and the Eagles blasted through our apartment one summer night when I was 9, and the neighbors called the police to report the noise. This was not the first time, but it was significantly different than before. The police had come to remove my sisters and me from the home. My mother was surprisingly docile. Joni hid and made her escape through an upstairs window. Kylene was away spending the night with friends. I was scared and didn't know what was going on. I hadn't thought of hiding or escaping as Joni had done.

"It's just going to be for the night," one of the cops told me, trying to calm me. "Just until your mother sobers up."

I had no way of knowing that one night would turn into months.

"C'mon, son," he said, taking my hand.

I tried to pull away, but he held on.

My mom stopped him, swept me into her arms and kissed me. "I love you, Kenan."

The police dragged me out of our apartment in the middle of the night and put me in the back of their squad car with nothing but the clothes I was wearing. I pressed my hands against the back window as my eyes welled up with tears. I stared, horrified, at my mother. As we drove off and she disappeared in the distance, I wondered if I'd ever see her again.

I discovered later that when the authorities caught up

to my sisters, they were taken away, too. We were now considered wards of the State. This was the first in a series of upheavals that would tear my family apart.

I was placed in a foster home. Joni and Kylene were kept together in another home. The people I stayed with seemed nice enough. The house was bigger than our apartment. The couple had children of their own and many other foster kids. We all got along pretty well, but it wasn't home, and they weren't my family.

Before I was able to get a toe-hold in these foreign surroundings, the State handed me over to a new foster family because there were too many children — 17 in all — in the Grangers' household.

The Palmers lived in a double-wide trailer, and they, too, had children, but not as many. Even though this house was smaller, I had more fun there. They had a cabin out in Willow and took all the children camping during the summer. They also owned a Beanie Baby shop in town, and I would go by frequently after school just to hang around until they closed — sometimes we'd even order pizza. No matter how much I liked it, sooner or later I felt I would be moved again because they began to acquire more foster children.

After the Palmers, I was placed with an aunt and uncle in Hooper Bay; but as soon as the caseworker came sniffing around and asking questions about the living arrangements, I was displaced again because the caseworker discovered that drugs were being used in the home.

OUT OF THE SHADOWS

In a relatively short span of time, I was bounced around between no fewer than four homes between Anchorage, Chevak and Hooper Bay.

I don't know how it happened, but for a time the State placed both Kylene, who was now 13, and me in the care of my brother Charles. Joni was sent to a different foster family in Anchorage where she'd stayed before. Charles lived on his own by then and had a 3-month-old son. We never spoke about what it was like to be the casualties of so much transition. We just accepted it for what it was.

As more time passed, I was finally allowed unsupervised visits with my mother, once a week for two hours. It wasn't ideal, but at least it was something.

We'd go to the mall food court to eat, and then we'd walk to my favorite store there, Northwind Kites. She'd buy me novelty toys like a small pair of binoculars, Mexican jumping beans and a whoopee cushion.

There were quite a few occasions when we'd just hang around her apartment and watch movies and television together.

Once, when she was out of the room, I inflated the whoopee cushion and slipped it under the blanket on the couch where she was sitting. It was all I could do to contain myself when she came back and sat on it. She was startled, and I erupted with laughter. It was good to laugh. Being with her reminded me of when I was 4 and she and I enjoyed what felt like our secret special time when she started teaching me how to read.

"I miss you, Mom. When can I come home?"

She'd look at me sadly and simply reply, "I don't know."

Mom stopped drinking by the time I was 12 years old. In 2003, Kylene and I were able to go back to live with her. Joni, who was six years older than me, stayed in Anchorage. The three of us moved to Chevak where I began seventh grade. I also began my own personal odyssey into hell.

⌒⌒⌒

While walking home from school one day, I felt a hard blow to the back of my head and lost my balance. My books scattered on the pavement in front of me. My hands instinctively thrust forward to catch myself as I fell. The glasses I wore slipped from my face and teetered on the tip of my nose.

"Hey, Bean Bag! Where ya headed?"

I pushed my glasses back in place and scrambled to collect my books. As I pulled up onto my knees, I felt a sharp kick to my abdomen and doubled over from the pain. Landing on my back, I curled up and wrapped my arms around myself. I squeezed my eyes shut as taunting laughter echoed around me. I could hear cars passing by on the street just a few feet away, but no one stopped to come to my rescue.

I was a reject — a castaway without a lot of friends, some Neanderthal's punching bag almost daily. Belittling names like *Bean Bag* and *Squidward* (because they thought my nose looked funny) and a few others that I can't mention were commonplace. Nothing about me escaped their ridicule — not even my mother. It had gotten so bad that I refused to go to school. But there was only one school in Chevak, so my choices were limited. School officials made excuses as to why they couldn't or wouldn't intervene. The only punishment my tormentors received was detention, which only fueled their ire and painted a bigger target on my back.

"Kenan, what's the matter? Why are you still in bed? Are you sick?"

"No."

"Then why are you crying?"

"I can't go back there."

"You can't go back where?"

"To that school. Please don't make me go back."

She was furious that the school had not taken action to prevent these assaults and confronted the principal.

"What do you mean there's nothing you can do about this? Are you blind or are you just stupid?! I can't believe that nobody here cares about the welfare of the students."

She was having none of that "boys will be boys" nonsense. It felt good to see my mother as my champion. However, her effort carried little weight. The bullying continued through the duration of the school year. Mostly in the lunch line they'd punch me in the back and grab food from my tray and run off to the amusement of all the other kids and a half-hearted reprimand from the teachers.

THE TRIUMPH OF NAPOLEON

At the world-weary age of 12, I was introduced to the mind-numbing sensation of marijuana, courtesy of Derek, who was my sister's boyfriend at the time.

"C'mon, try it," he urged, smirking. "You'll get used to it. It's not that bad."

I was initially apprehensive, but I watched how he did it, putting the funny-looking paper-enwrapped herb to his lips and inhaling the pungent aroma. He languidly leaned back on the sofa in his apartment and passed the joint to me. "Man, this is good stuff."

It didn't appear to be that big a deal. I looked at it, then back to him and slowly raised it to my lips. Turns out I didn't like it at all. In fact, I choked, coughed and threw up. As I gasped for a clean breath, Derek laughed — reminding me of the taunting I received at school.

Like most families that deal with addiction, drugs and alcohol were a lethal combination. My older brother Christian committed suicide by a drug overdose when he was only 25 years old. Two days after Christmas in 2003, my mom called the hospital my brother was staying at to say hi to him, only to discover he had died. For weeks I tried to make sense of what Christian had done. I agonized over the thought of what I could have done to make a difference. Could I have called him more? Could I have said anything to persuade him to move to Chevak with us? There are always the *what ifs* and *if onlys* that accompany devastation, but never any real answers. The upside, if you can call it that, is that the bullying let up for a while. It was as if the universe held back the fists of fury to allow me to grieve.

Another change came in 2004. My mom was beginning a new chapter in her life and wanted to go back to school for business management. Leaving the now-adult Joni and Kylene behind, we made the trek east to Fairbanks, where we stayed for nine months.

After the completion of my mother's course work, we traveled back to Anchorage, where we moved in with my sister Joni, her boyfriend and their 3-year-old son, Andrew. Joni lived in the same neighborhood I knew as a kid. The stench of familiarity enveloped me as we seemingly took a step back in time. I had to repeat the eighth grade because we'd done so much jumping around that I'd missed the last three months of the previous school year.

That would have been upsetting enough, but what made it worse was the fact that no one on the home front had a job, which was a recipe for disaster. Crowded living conditions resulted in escalating tension, which caused Joni's boyfriend to move out. Four short months after we settled in, we were evicted for non-payment of the rent.

With nowhere else to go, my mom moved into a motel, and I was allowed to stay with a classmate who lived with his grandparents. They liked me, but during this period, I felt pressured by my friend to experiment with marijuana — and this time she came with a little friend called pornography.

THE TRIUMPH OF NAPOLEON

I didn't have a girlfriend at the time, but I started getting a lot of unwanted attention from older women. Their wanton gazes and salacious smirks caused me a great deal of angst as I was not prepared for the expectations they implied.

A particular incident I flashed on was when one of my mom's friends came to visit. I had come in after playing, and she was gathering her things to leave. The woman looked at me strangely and smiled. It sounded like she asked me if she could "have some." I was an inexperienced 14 year old, and I wasn't quite sure, so with wide-eyed amazement I asked, "What did you say?" She put her hand on my shoulder and leaned into me. Nervously, I jerked away. I never told anyone. She didn't come around much after that.

My cousin's 16-year-old girlfriend was much more vocal about her intentions. She approached me one day when he was not within earshot and brazenly whispered what she wanted to do to me sexually. She addressed me as Mr. Napoleon. I assumed she was joking, but the leer in her eyes said differently. I ignored the seduction. For fear of incurring my cousin's wrath, or possibly having the situation turned against me, I never told him — and I don't think she did, either.

Watching these images on the screen stirred confusion and uneasiness. My body was aroused with overwhelming desires that I didn't know what to do with. I didn't know who I was anymore or why I indulged in the things that I did. The landscape of my future was starting to feel as stark and as cold as the tundra. This was not the place for me, physically or emotionally, and all I could do was bide my time until the next move.

చ్చిచ్చిచ్చి

Homesick, my mom and I flew back to Chevak after a month and a half, where we stayed with friends. I began the ninth grade in 2006, and you'll never guess what happened — there were bullies there, too! I had read the words of God in the Bible: "Vengeance is mine. I will repay" (Romans 12:19). For some reason, I held onto that notion and still never fought back. It didn't help that I was becoming adept at smoking pot. I didn't fight that, either.

Eventually my mom decided to attend AVTEC (Alaska Vocational Technical Center) in the town of Seward, on the Kenai Peninsula, to study culinary arts. Afterward she worked in a couple of restaurants, while I remained with an aunt in Chevak for the next 11 months. I reunited with my mother in the summer of 2008.

Constant change had long become a way of life, whether out of necessity or not. After four weeks of no established roots and no place to stay, we moved on to the city of Kenai, but that was not yet the end of our sojourn. With each move there were a lot of things left unfinished; friendships forged through common interests and lost through brevity, church programs that offered promise but never panned out, simple boyhood pleasures like building stock cars and racing — these were the events that allowed escape from the surreal world that had taken shape around me.

Mom found an apartment back in Seward, and that is where I finally completed my junior and senior years of high school. I also participated in the Native Youth Olympics, where nearly 400 youth from across Alaska assembled to demonstrate their skills in traditional Native games.

There were events like the Eskimo Stick Pull, a game where hand, back and leg strength are essential. Successful hunters must be able to pull a seal out of the water, no easy task while maintaining balance on snow and ice. Then there was the One-Hand Reach, a game to test a person's control over his body. If a hunter was to become lost on water, for example, he must know the skills to control his body in order not to panic and tip his kayak. The Seal Hop was a game of sheer endurance to see how far a person can go on pure determination. This game originated from the hunter imitating the movement of a seal during the hunt.

There also was the Kneel Jump, similar to the Scissor Broad Jump in that the hunters must develop the skill of quick movement to be successful in jumping from one ice floe to another. This game also develops leg muscles necessary to lift heavy game and carry it back to the village. And then there was the One-Foot High Kick, a traditional jumping event at many Arctic sports competitions. In the One-Foot High Kick, athletes must jump using two feet, touch a hanging target with one foot and land on the foot they kicked with, maintaining balance. The event is often considered the most demanding Arctic sport. This was my favorite.

For a time, things seemed normal — or at least bore the façade of normalcy.

෧෧෧

A bout with alcoholism and a massive seizure claimed Joni's life in 2009. The irony that she died at the age of 25, just like my brother Christian, was almost impossible to comprehend. I sank into depression again, crying, forcing myself to eat and thinking of the 7-year-old son she left behind. If the loss of my oldest brother and sister has taught me anything at all, it is to love and value those around me and not to take anyone or anything for granted.

Some time after coping with Joni's death, my mom found Eagle's Nest Christian Fellowship in Seward.

She had an affinity toward it because of its former name, Seward Assembly of God. I was initially reluctant when she asked me to go with her. Then I figured, *What did I have to lose?* We were both searching for something other than alcohol or pot to alleviate our anguish; we might as well give God a shot.

It was a pretty cool experience. The church wasn't over-the-top charismatic, but the singing and the worship were definitely a draw that my heart connected to almost immediately. A few months after we started going, the church hosted what they called a Youth Explosion, and suddenly, as if it was what I'd been waiting for, I was home. No more wandering like a nomad or being tossed about like a Frisbee. I found myself at home, responding to the call to surrender my life to Jesus.

One Sunday after service, I was approached by the youth pastor, Jorge Alvial, who asked me if I wanted to be a youth leader. I had no idea what all that entailed, but it sounded interesting enough to explore. There was a three-month training period as I prepared to take on this new challenge in my life. I was given an opportunity to lead a discussion group for the youth on sharing in the suffering of Christ. I suppose I had a real personal connection to the theme, since I was no stranger to suffering and really identified with the idea of being rejected.

I was baptized in Resurrection Bay in 2010. Being a part of the Invictus Youth Movement gave me a sense of purpose and identity that I hadn't known before. And since I've always been fascinated by technology since first learning how to program a VCR at 2 years old, I'm now involved with the sound and video department of the church. Had I finally stumbled upon God's plan for me?

ॐॐॐ

In 1857, the English poet William Earnest Henley penned the ode *Invictus*. One of the most compelling stanzas reads as follows:

OUT OF THE SHADOWS

I thank whatever gods may be
For my unconquerable soul.
In the fell clutch of circumstance
I have not winced nor cried aloud
Under the bludgeonings of chance
My head is bloodied, but not bowed.

Every feeling of rejection and confusion I'd ever internalized was only to build my character. I'm still discovering all there is for me at Eagle's Nest Christian Fellowship, and I don't know yet what I will be. But I know that all the loss and pain was somehow meant for my good, just as it says in Romans 8:28: "And we know that all things work together for good to them that love God, to them who are called according to his purpose."

God had been waiting just for me. Not too shabby for a punching bag.

MAXIMUM SECURITY
The Story of Sharon
Written by Christee Wise

"Come to Alaska with me," he said.

"What?"

"Yeah, we get along pretty good. We could both use a fresh start."

A fresh start? I wanted nothing more.

I loathed myself for what I was doing. I'd been caring for Gerald, my third husband, for three years since he was hit by a car and suffered extensive brain damage. Before the accident, his addictions to drugs and alcohol controlled our lives. Our limited income evaporated as soon as we earned it.

My sense of obligation to Gerald had faded some in the absence of love, but my boys and I had no place else to go. I had no choice but to find additional work.

"I can get you work," Paula promised.

I resisted. "I don't think I …"

"Listen, you don't have to go out on a street corner or anything. You just come over to the house, and I'll make all the arrangements," she pressed. I didn't think to ask her what she got out of the deal. With my back against a wall and my soul stripped bare, I reluctantly agreed.

I was relieved when Andy, one of the Johns, hired me to work in his automotive shop answering the phone, bookkeeping and delivering parts.

Andy pledged his loyalty and proposed a new start in a new place, Alaska. I wanted to believe he could give me that and provide the kind of love and security I wanted most for me and my sons.

I'd have traded anything to recover a smidgen of my self-worth.

❧ ❧ ❧

Dottie was tagging orders when I arrived. I'd been working after school at the dry cleaners since my sophomore year in high school. Seeing several bins of laundry waiting to be processed, I started sorting shirts and pants. Dottie was 18, just a couple years older than I was, but she imagined herself far more mature and experienced.

"What's wrong with you?" she quizzed me haughtily. "Long day at high school?"

I'd been struggling since I got back from a retreat the previous weekend. During the retreat, I started to feel guilty because the parochial school I attended frowned on dating. I broke up with my boyfriend when we got back.

Days after the retreat and breakup, I noticed looks of disdain from my female classmates and whispers and grins from the boys. "She's easy," I overheard earlier that day.

My face burned with humiliation, and tears stung my eyes. I barely made it through my classes and was still seething when I arrived at "One-Hour Martinizing," face-to-face with Dottie the Great.

"You? Easy?" Dottie laughed. "You wouldn't know the first thing to do with a guy. You'd probably just lie there."

I bristled at the implication and smartly defended myself. "I know more than you think I do."

I refused to give her the satisfaction of thinking I didn't know about sex, whether I did or not. I put my shoulders back and stalked away, pretending that I had work in the back room.

Dottie's remark really got under my skin, scraping past wounds infected by put-downs and hurts of a childhood lost amid 14 other struggling family members, counting parents and children.

My angry inner battle mounted on my next few dates. I practically had to fight the guys off with my fists. I was small, and they probably saw me as an easy target. The rumors hadn't helped. One guy I had heard was a perfect gentleman, but on our date his pawing advances sent me climbing over the seat of the car to get away. I didn't have sex with any of them, not even the steady who claimed I had gone all the way with him.

The real truth about my purity cowered deep inside of my heart, showing itself only to me in unguarded moments. I could hide it, but I couldn't forget it.

ৡৡৡ

Ascending the stairs to my father's office, I carried a single hope like a treasure — that he would notice and love me just for being me. One of 10 children born to a

USAF pilot POW of the Second World War, I wasn't favored by being first or last in the birth order. A tender heart made me especially vulnerable, and I longed just to know I was valued as his one and only 10 year old at that moment.

I tapped lightly on the door. "Good night, Daddy. It's Sharon."

He usually kept it latched, even locked, but it swung open a little, and I saw that he was lying on the single bed opposite his big desk. I never understood why he had a bed separate from the one that he shared with my mother.

I looked at his face for my next cue. Expressionless, he stared back, as if trying to remember who I was. He motioned me over to him. "Close the door, and come here."

I obeyed.

My father terrified me. He'd used a switch on me only once that I could remember, along with my younger brother Mitchell, because we kept climbing on the bumper of the car.

But I'd seen him beat my siblings black and blue plenty of times with whatever was handy. Once he beat Mitchell for something that I did, but I was too afraid to tell him I was the one who took the key to his office and got it stuck in the lock.

My father reached for my hand, and I automatically reached back to take his.

He took my hand and pulled me onto the bed. My stomach instantly turned with indescribable dread. He wasn't playing. My father never played. I'd never even seen him wrestle with my brothers.

He began to pull at my nightgown. Fear siphoned the strength from my limbs and cut off my breath. Too terrified to speak or to move, I let him do what he wanted. My head swam and my heart pounded, but I lay perfectly still and silent as he molested me completely.

When he finally released me, I lay paralyzed with shock and revulsion. Then he delivered his nonchalant conclusion of what he implied was a complete and appropriate checkup of all things female and 10 years old: "Yep, you're okay."

And then without so much as uttering my name, he excused me from his presence. Weakly I rose and robotically left the room.

I never again approached my father for any reason.

ॐॐॐ

"Do you think you're having a boy or a girl this time?"

"Well, Sharon was *supposed* to be a boy." I heard my name and my mother's answer, as though the statement explained everything. I blinked and suppressed the twinge in my heart. I was young enough and in a large enough family to feel a slight gratification at first that my name would be mentioned in Mother's conversation.

But her words were pregnant with meaning and heavy to me. In two or three months, she would deliver my third younger brother or sister. The birth of each new sibling gave the other members of my family a reason to repeat the story about me.

My father piloted a fighter plane during World War II. He was shot down, captured and held in a German prison camp until the end of the war. He missed the birth of my brother Teddy, their second child. The war ended that year, and my dad was released. He returned and continued his military career, but not as a pilot. Shortly after his return, Mother became pregnant and had a second baby girl, my sister Ricki, short for Victoria.

Mother was pregnant with baby number four when Father received orders that they would be shipped to England. My mother's younger brother, Robby, came to Illinois for a long visit before the growing family prepared to move overseas.

Teddy adored his 16-year-old uncle. Sandwiched between two sisters, the 5 year old soaked up Uncle Robby's attention like a thirsty sponge.

"Girl, boy, girl …" Uncle Robby prompted Teddy. "I think your mommy needs to have another boy, don't you?"

"Yeah!" Teddy grinned toothlessly. He felt empowered by his uncle's attention to make his wish for a brother come true simply by declaration.

Uncle Robby laughed. "Yep! What this family needs is more men," he growled playfully. He gave Teddy a bear hug and wrestled him to the floor.

Before my arrival, everyone was convinced I needed to be a boy in order to keep the pattern even. My father wasn't present at my birth, and when he was informed I was a girl, he nicknamed me "The Little Disappointment."

Following his brother-in-law's lead and identifying with "poor Teddy," Uncle Robby helped Teddy make a sign for my bassinette. The word was long and hard to spell, but they pieced together sheets of paper and carefully squeezed all the letters onto the banner:

D-I-S-A-P-P-O-I-N-T-M-E-N-T.

Of course, I couldn't read or understand the inscription on the bed that had received three babies before me, including Theodore, with much less ceremony. But each time I heard the story I was a little bit older and absorbed the subtle references with new depths of painful understanding. In sing-song voice, one of my siblings inevitably added, "Yeah, your name was gonna be Richard Earle."

The contempt of the male members of my family sealed my value based upon my gender. My father showed little interest in any of us, but I grew particularly wary of drawing negative attention. The threat of unleashing his merciless teasing and scorn petrified me.

Like father, like son. Teddy hardly spoke to me, especially as we got older. When I was a preschooler, he invited me to play with him. But I didn't like the way he touched me when we played. I was always terribly afraid that we would get caught, and I'd be the one punished.

Sarcasm pervaded our home. I despised being singled out for ridicule or blame. Wherever this sensitivity originated, it made me a target for just the treatment I earnestly tried to avoid. I hated being ignored but accepted it as a lesser evil than being the butt of a joke or a scapegoat.

St. Mary's Academy loomed like an enormous monster ready to swallow me on my first day of school. Now that I was old enough to go to school, I walked by myself. My three older siblings ran ahead to join their friends. No one held my hand or lingered with me while I learned the name of the strict-looking nun who would be my teacher. She was much taller than my mama, and the long black habit covered every soft part of her. From the hair on her head to her toes, she was hidden. Even the expression on her pale cream face masked something, perhaps an injured tenderness disposed to small children.

Father Patrick frightened me the most. He, too, was more like a giant robed shadow than a human being. I stood wide-eyed on the playground teeming with children of all sizes, shapes and ages. Father Patrick suddenly stepped up beside me and scooped me into his arms.

"Here, let me hold you up so you can see," he boomed as he hoisted me above the crowd. "You're so little!" His deep voice startled me and rang out for everyone to hear.

I did not care to see anything from this vantage point. Frightened senseless, I stiffened in his arms. Every voice quieted, every face turned to look, every jump rope and ball halted. Hundreds of eyes stared and hundreds of ears heard that I was the smallest person in the entire school. Laughter echoed in my ears, filling the silence and bouncing from the stone walls of the church and school. I reddened in mortified embarrassment. Finally, Father Patrick set me down. My feet barely hit the ground and I bolted through the crowd, dodging astonished students and surprised nuns. I ran blindly until I could go no farther. I crawled into a nearby stairwell and cried inconsolably.

Had I not been forced, dragged out from under the stairs by another harsh-featured nun, I'd have never returned. And if I hadn't remembered the humiliating event, my schoolmates kept it fresh, calling me "Shorty" for the rest of my school years.

I'm a misfit, I declared to myself. *I don't even look like anyone in my family.* I wanted so much to belong somewhere, to find acceptance in the group, whether within my family or elsewhere.

৵৵৵

What difference does it make? I thought. The cutting remarks from high school classmates eroded my will to save myself. *If everybody thinks I'm having sex, why not?*

My decaying self-image absorbed the notion. My pride scrambled to keep up. I vowed, *The next time a date tries something, I'm going to find out what all the fuss is about.*

Unparalleled disappointment in myself and in the experience ambushed me after I had sex the first time. Physical intimacy without true love and relationship weakened the boundaries of my heart and laid it open to thieves. Shame and guilt held me tightly in their grip.

From that day, I sought love and acceptance by giving guys the only thing I thought might entice them to care about me. What I thought would fill my need for relationship destroyed me instead.

Catholicism suffocated me. My father's hypocrisy strangled my faith in men and in God. I transferred to public school my junior year and continued recklessly acting out until I became pregnant right before graduation.

"You whore!" my father raged, flinging his hands in the air and stomping a confined circuit of the living room.

Mother balanced my baby sister on her hip and tried to stay on her feet with a 3 year old climbing her other leg. She began to cry.

My parents didn't ask about the boy. I wondered why but guessed it didn't matter. We'd only dated a time or two. He used me and discarded me like all the rest. And he certainly didn't want a kid. He offered to give me money to fly out of state and get an abortion. I wanted nothing to do with him as soon as I heard his repugnant offer.

"Well, you can't stay here," they concluded.

"H***, no!" my father added.

They couldn't bear what the neighbors might think. I supposed that included everyone in the Catholic church — the priests, the nuns who taught me in school. By this time, my father had retired from the military and was teaching school in the parish in Kansas where we had finally settled somewhat. With 13 kids and grandchildren on the way, we were well known within the community.

MAXIMUM SECURITY

My mother hardly spoke about my predicament. Later, I realized that she, too, was afraid of my father. She was busy bearing and caring for children, 13 in all, and in her own monumental emotional battle to make it from one day to the next.

I was sent to live with Janie, my oldest sister, who was now married and pregnant with her second child.

Then Harvey reentered my life. Harvey and I had dated briefly when I was 16. He had asked me to marry him, and I told him no. I was not in love with Harvey or ready to get married.

"Sharon, I still want to marry you," he told me the first time we saw each other again.

"I'm pregnant."

"I know. We need each other. The baby needs a father," he replied as he launched his case.

I didn't know what to tell him. No woman that I knew had ever raised a baby by herself. I needed a husband.

Janie and I were never close. But as I'd been thrust into her home, pregnant and unmarried, I guardedly confided in my oldest sister. She changed a diaper as we talked.

"Do you love him?" She turned to look at me while keeping one hand on the baby. She held up a diaper pin.

I took the pin from her, opened it and handed it back before answering. "I can learn to love."

Harvey was the logical solution to my dilemma. We were married, and I determined to make the best of it for my baby's sake. My pride committed me to live with my decisions.

OUT OF THE SHADOWS

My husband's domineering ways and heavy-handedness surfaced after we were married and when he drank heavily. The more booze he poured into his system, the more rage poured out.

I followed my mother's model and tolerated his bad behavior for the first five years. *He's not so bad when he's sober. I made my bed; I'm going to have to sleep in it. Life is not a bowl of cherries.*

He hit and pushed me occasionally, but I reasoned that I probably deserved it. *I'll just have to try to stay out of his way when he's been drinking. Let him rant.*

I tried to interrupt an angry tirade by taking my toddler from the kitchen to the living room one evening. Michael clung to my leg, making it hard to move. Harvey stumbled along behind screaming belligerently, "Don't you walk away from me, b****!"

I bent to pick Michael up to comfort and protect him, hoping Harvey might back off a little for his sake. But before I could get my hands around the child, Harvey shoved me hard to the couch.

Maternal instinct collided with the end of my patience, and I exploded. I bounced off the couch and stood face-to-face with a surprised Harvey. He sneered and shoved me back to the couch. "Yer gonna sit there, and yer gonna listen to me, 'cuz yer my wife!" he screamed.

Michael had begun to cry, and I buckled on the couch again. The child shrieked and wailed even louder. Boiling mad, I rebounded from the couch to face Harvey. "I am not!"

He bellowed and pushed me down again.

"B******!" I stood up and screamed in his face.

Instantly, his hands went around my throat, and he lunged, sending me backward against the back cushions of the couch and over the top. My head and shoulders shattered the front window as together we plunged headlong into it.

Michael still clung to my leg, trembling and screaming.

I decided that I couldn't just learn to love someone like this. I certainly could die trying, and I didn't want that for my kids. I had to work two jobs to support myself and the two boys I then had. I found a modest low-rent apartment, and we at least seemed safe in our own house when I was home.

One night, though, as the boys slept in the next room, a stranger broke into the apartment, attacked, beat and raped me. He left me bloodied and violated in my own bedroom.

I directed all of my energy toward providing for and protecting my boys. Although romantic relationships were secondary, I usually had a steady with whom I regularly engaged in sex.

I managed to scrape together the money to buy my son a bicycle for his birthday. My neighbor Rodney offered to help assemble it. I knew that Rodney was engaged to the woman who lived in the apartment below me. And he knew that I had a boyfriend. But after I put the boys to bed one evening, he came over, and we tackled the project together.

"Would you like some wine?" I offered as he spread the instructions out on the floor.

"Sure," he answered casually.

He'd begun to read the directions and sort parts when I handed him a glass. We sipped wine and laughed as we tried to separate rights and lefts, identify parts A, B, C and D and distinguish bolts that differed by mere millimeters.

I kept refilling our empty glasses, and we continued to work and to sip and to laugh. Our hands brushed each other, and we let them remain longer than necessary. We warmed to one another, and as he reached for a wrench, we paused face-to-face just an inch or two apart. Then we burst into laughter, casually dismissed our loyalty to the others and gave in to base desire.

I stared at myself in the mirror. Sickness rose in my throat. I'd censored the truth for three weeks as days passed without a trace of my period. I turned away from my own reflection and dissolved into tears. *It can't be Steven's — he can't have children.*

I crumpled to the bedroom floor, wrapping my arms around my stomach. Razor-sharp truth cut into my heart, and pain pumped through the rest of my body. The one-night stand with Rodney yielded the conception of a child I could never care for. I convulsed in hopelessness.

The father of my oldest had offered to pay to get rid of our problem, but since then I had never considered abortion an option.

It's my only option, I thought anew. Immediately I was overwhelmed with shame and grief.

Rodney was not interested whatsoever in supporting a child. I could not afford another child, since I was barely able to feed and clothe the two I had.

After the abortion, I pushed my reprehensible behavior out of my mind. I returned to the business of surviving the next day, week, month, year, trying to keep food on the table and the gnawing emptiness in my life from devouring me.

Eventually, I grew tired of being alone and married again. The mysterious vortex of abuse sucked me into the role of a victim of an abusive alcoholic all over again. Unable to perform, my husband sexually assaulted me with objects. Within a year, he beat me too many times to count and exposed me to a life-threatening cervical cancer.

I married Gerald next. The accident changed both of our lives.

Andy promised a new beginning in Alaska, but his plan didn't include a clean break from his past. Andy bounced back and forth between his wife and children in the Lower 48 and me and mine in Anchorage. I lived in denial for a few years. But I was hardly surprised to discover his infidelity, since I had been his mistress in the beginning. We officially ended the marriage after 13 years.

On rare occasions in my darkest days, I sought refuge in the church. Although I visited a number of Protestant churches, I never counted myself worthy of the very hope and comfort I wanted so much to find. I often slipped in and out of the congregation, trying to be loved without being seen. And usually I dropped out after a couple of weeks or so.

అంఅంఅం

I couldn't sleep. Finally, sometime after 1 a.m., I slipped from under the covers and left my sleeping husband's side. Just enough light from above the stove in the kitchen spilled out into the adjoining hall and rooms to prevent me from stumbling over the few furnishings. Worn out from crying but unable to sleep, I paced about the small rooms.

A pile of bills lay on the corner of the dining table where I had tossed them earlier. The red ink seemed to glow in the dark: "Final Notice, Overdue, Urgent!" Another tidal wave of guilt and fear crashed against my weakened nerves, and I buckled and caught myself on the back of a nearby chair. Not only were we falling further behind on our bills, but we were arguing more frequently about money. This was my fifth marriage, and I didn't want to fail again or to lose Jack.

"What can I do?" I sobbed into the silence. "I can't do this anymore."

The futility of my circumstances, *our* circumstances, leveled a final crushing blow to my spirit in the pre-dawn hours, and I collapsed on the sofa. For several minutes, I wept. My heart ached so much I thought it would stop altogether. And I nearly prayed for the relief that death might bring.

MAXIMUM SECURITY

Trapped in a cycle of unconsciously bad choices, I'd at many times considered suicide my only way out. I was unsuccessful even in that. Was God so disappointed in me that he would punish me like this forever?

My crying subsided to pinched-off gulps of air. Absentmindedly, I picked up a book I hadn't noticed lying on the coffee table before. I fanned the pages with my right hand while I mopped my face with a tissue in my left. The name of a well-known actress caught my eye, and I began to read her story, just to distract myself from my own misery. I finished her story and went on to the next one about a pro athlete and others whose lives were transformed when they surrendered themselves to God.

God had always frightened me, much like my earthly father. I desperately desired to know him, but I feared him in his role as heavenly father. The title translated to me a cosmic judge waiting to crush me, someone so great and so holy that he wanted little to do with me. I truly wanted to come close to him, but was deathly afraid of him.

God appeared as love and mercy in all the stories I read that night in that little book. I understood his judgment as right and just and holy, but my focus turned to his all-inclusive love. All of a sudden, the most horrifying thing I could imagine wasn't that I might burn in hell for my sin, but that I would be eternally separated from the one soul that was capable of loving me without reservation, condition or end.

Abuse, homelessness, bankruptcy, pain, sickness, even abject poverty suddenly held no threat at all to me. A new awareness consumed my consciousness, that God was near enough to touch, but if I didn't reach out to him, the opportunity would slip through my fingers forever. The prospect filled me with dread, and I buried my face in the couch as I cried out to God to take me as I was.

"God," I begged, "give me a chance to devote myself to you alone." I followed "The Sinner's Prayer" in the back of the book, asking God to "forgive me of my sin and come into my heart."

Time stood still. I felt new strength and confidence seeping into my heart, along with a determination I'd never had before. He was willing to wipe out my past. I was willing to start again. A rush of love surged up from the bottom of my heart.

I saw myself in a new light, the light of God's love. His love provided the security I needed to take an honest look at myself. Habits and behaviors to which I'd never paid attention stood out in stark opposition to the newfound light and love in my heart.

I heard a woman cursing a blue streak on the plane in a seat behind me and realized, *I sound like that.* I noticed the provocative outfits of other women and thought, *I look and act like that.* Instead of the unrelenting guilt and condemnation I had felt before, I couldn't wait to rid myself of those patterns. I knew I would find in him everything that I needed.

I brought Christ into my home, though my husband wasn't interested in hearing about it. Often he'd ridicule me or bring up mistakes I had made to try to discredit my faith. But faithfulness to God meant faithfulness to my marriage, no matter what the circumstances. Faith in God meant trusting him to provide, even when my husband was out of work or made choices I didn't agree with.

☙☙☙

Layer by layer, God gently peeled back the hurt and bitterness, the defenses I'd put up and the shame I wore like heavy coverings.

The women in the ladies' Bible study I attended were talking about "the voice of God." They each told stories of times that God had spoken to them. Old feelings of inferiority surfaced because I had never received such a message from the Lord or heard his voice. I longed for a transformational experience like that.

I wanted to do everything right. Like a toddler in my faith, I was young and impressionable, eager to please the Lord. I was just learning to walk and kept bumping into obstacles, tripping and sometimes falling over.

I'd come upon some difficulties in my life and felt terribly alone. A teaching that I'd recently received said that a Christian should find a spiritual mentor to look to as a father or mother. I accepted this instruction without question. *I have to find someone like this,* I thought.

After hours of prayer, I decided that God would have me ask a certain pastor and his wife to guide me in this way. I invited the pastor's wife to lunch and confided my deepest feelings. "I don't feel I have ever been truly loved."

Suddenly, the woman was beside herself. She put down her napkin, canceled her lunch and left the restaurant, obviously offended by what she perceived as a personal attack.

Later, I went to her house and tried to explain, to no avail. And when I met with the pastor to try to straighten out the misunderstanding, he, too, was insulted and reprimanded me for several other unrelated issues.

Crushing rejection and heartbreaking shame bore down on me. Once again, I had knocked at my father's door to talk with him and was yanked into a chamber of horrors. Utterly betrayed, I poured my broken heart out to God in sobs because my sorrow was too deep for words.

I managed only to get through the barest routine the next couple of days. Then, as I stood in the kitchen alone, I heard a sudden unmistakable pronouncement:

"I WILL NEVER LEAVE YOU NOR FORSAKE YOU!"

Each word was announced with clarity and emphasis. I knew it was the Lord speaking. The voice was audible and loud. I turned, and there was no one in the room with me.

And then I heard it repeated, each of the first three words punctuated for effect.

"I ..." I knew it was God speaking.

"WILL ..." he promised.

"NEVER ..." What men had done to me over and over was impossible for him: "LEAVE YOU NOR FORSAKE YOU."

I burst into a new round of tears, grateful tears for

God's attentiveness and care — for me, so undeserving, so desperate.

At the time, both my husband and I were self-employed. Each day brought new struggles to make ends meet. I provided residential care for disabled people, but I'd also taken a newspaper delivery route to bring in additional income. Alone in my car, I cherished moments of companionship with the Lord who had so unmistakably spoken to me. I carefully loaded the CD changer in my car to alternate between discs of Christian music and the Bible read aloud on CD.

About two or three weeks had passed since the Lord had spoken to me in the kitchen. Changes in my lifestyle and behavior were occurring in rapid succession. I connected with a women's Bible study in the community and realized the power of friendship, sharing my needs and concerns and praying for the needs and concerns of others.

One morning, I wove through the dark, wintry roads around Seward delivering the paper. I sang to the God I'd come to know not as an angry father, but as one who loves us with the purest form of unconditional love that exists. Tears of overwhelming appreciation and love for the Savior began to spill from my eyes and splash on the plastic-wrapped newspaper lying across my lap.

The tears turned to weeping, and my heart was seized with the pressure of God's love for all people. In particular, I sensed God's heart longing for those that may be least deserving of his love and forgiveness. Overcome to the point of impairment, I maneuvered the car to the side of the snowy street. With the motor still running, I gripped the steering wheel with both hands and dropped my forehead to rest on the curve between them.

Moved by God's mercy toward me, I prayed, "God, let me love the unlovable."

The warm wave of love rushed over and through me. "Simply love."

☙ ☙ ☙

"You should go to work at the prison," my husband had stated matter-of-factly a few weeks earlier.

"Really?"

"Yes, it would be a great job. The benefits, the schedule. I'm done with this assisted living thing. You need to find something else."

My friend had applied, and I considered working in corrections but not seriously until Jack mentioned it. At the time, he was very protective of me. When I realized he was not only supportive but in favor of my working for the Department of Corrections at the all-male maximum-security prison in Seward, I applied.

The intense multiple-stage application and screening process was taking up to months and sometimes more. My application flew through the system in half the time. Just five months after I prayed, asking God to help me to love people that were hard to love, I was called in for training. A 55-year-old grandmother, I showed my I.D. at the entrance. I submitted to a security check and waited for the last set of steel-barred doors to slide open. I stepped inside, and the doors slid closed behind me.

The briefest shiver of anxiety ran through me and was gone instantly. From that first moment, love chased away all the fear.

Hurt and anger and even fear pervade the interior of a prison. Correction officers and inmates alike fight their own private battles with disappointment, loss, trials and pain, both physical and emotional. The mandate I received to "simply love" stayed with me.

For security reasons, we are not allowed to touch the inmates. I cannot hug them, though sometimes it's what I feel led to do. I cannot tell them outright about the love of God and his desire to draw them into his own arms.

Raymond, an inmate the same age as my oldest grandson and likely still growing, towered over me. Anger radiated from the golden brown skin on his neck and arms. Mammoth muscles rippled beneath its tawny surface. He was tough enough when he'd been sentenced for the murder of another teenager. But his heart had become even harder.

I tipped my head back and looked straight into eyes so dark the pupils disappeared into the larger circles. I saw a little boy, falling backward into black emptiness, his face pale with fear, bitterness and desperation.

At 18, he faced a life sentence in a maximum-security facility. Going nowhere, doing nothing, without purpose. Instead of shrinking in fear, my own heart melted with tenderness toward the lost child.

I stood 5 foot, 1 inch to his 6-feet-plus height. I weighed 118 pounds; he weighed twice that, plus some. But I couldn't help the smile that spread across my face or the love that flowed out of my heart like a rushing fountain.

"What are you lookin' at?" he asked suspiciously.

Without hesitation, I answered. "You, Raymond. God just wants you to know that he sees you. He is so pleased with you. You are on the right track."

Surprise flickered in his eyes, and his features softened before he stopped himself. He let out a contemptuous, "Geez!" and turned away.

I didn't see him for several weeks and gave little thought to the encounter. I spoke the words that God had given me at the time and believed that he would do as he pleased with them.

My heart broke for the teens in the Youth Offender Pod, the section set aside primarily for teenaged inmates. General population is added to the youth offender section as necessary due to overcrowding. I requested that I be assigned to the Youth Offender Pod more permanently.

"I wouldn't want my wife working here," Mel, one of the senior officers, commented.

I understood that my size and gender may not inspire confidence. But I had complete confidence in the Lord.

"There is someone very big right behind me," I explained, as I had just told an inmate. "You will never see him unless you mess with me."

The prisoner blinked, breaking the hard stare he'd focused on me. "I believe you." He held up his hands and grinned.

The officer shook his head and turned away.

Native Alaskan culture reveres grandparents, and many of the residents of the prison were raised by grandparents. One youth offender called me "Grandma," and it caught on. Other officers tried to quell the trend until I said that I didn't mind. The term spoke respect and honor to me.

I requested to be assigned to the Youth Offender Pod a second time. I had worked there several years earlier for a brief time and wished to stay. The position was given to someone else who seemed to the supervisors to better fit the profile they preferred. But after several months, the gentleman who met the criteria and was selected decided he didn't want to work there anymore.

"I want to put you back in the Youth Offender Pod," my supervisor announced. What I had not been able to do naturally in many months, God accomplished in moments. I've been working in the prison for seven years. God had been working on hearts and circumstances to bring about his will the entire time.

Coming off my shift, I met up with Mel, my relief in the Youth Offender Pod. We paused to talk. I always liked talking to Mel because he, too, was a Christian, and we frequently talked about the Lord and encouraged each other. I knew his family from church.

"Sharon, do you realize that since you and I are in this

section, there are four Christians working here? One per shift!" Mel noted.

Oh, how God loves us.

I know the provision of Christian workers in the area is for my good, as well as for the inmates.

"I thought you disapproved of women working here." I reminded Mel of his reference to his wife.

"Oh, but my wife is not you, and you are not my wife," he explained.

The warmth of God's love and affirmation swept over me.

"Grandma, anyone messes with you, we've got your back," one young man promised. Even though there are surveillance cameras that watch our every move, I gave him the sign for "hug." A great big grin spread across the teen's face, because I took the risk to speak his language.

Days later, Raymond approached me. "I have to tell you something, Grandma."

"What's that?"

"You'll never know how much what you said to me the other day meant to me. I was really feeling discouraged, and then you said that God wanted me to know I was on the right track."

"He really loves you, Raymond," I reminded him.

I saw a spark of life in his eye, though he nodded almost imperceptibly before he left me.

Many years before, I begged God to speak to me as he seemed to speak so plainly and profoundly to others. He answered with the command, "Simply love." He called, filled and then released me to love the unlovable. I may have been, to myself, the most unlovable of all.

"Who shall separate us from the love of Christ?
Shall trouble or hardship or persecution or famine
or nakedness or danger or sword?
As it is written: 'For your sake we face death all day long;
we are considered as sheep to be slaughtered.'
No, in all these things we are more than conquerors
through him who loved us.
For I am convinced that neither death nor life,
neither angels nor demons,
neither the present nor the future, nor any powers,
neither height nor depth, nor anything else in all
creation, will be able to separate us from the love
of God that is in Christ Jesus our Lord."
(Romans 8:35-39)

And from the maximum security of God's love, I chose, as my precious Lord Jesus did, simply to love.

REJECTION TO REJOICING
The Story of Mary Goodwater
Written by Anne C. Johnson

"Mommy, Mommy," I giggled.

"Oh, my little one," Mommy's soft voice cooed.

Her arms wrapped around me. Frizzy black hair strayed out from her cornrows and tickled my cheek. I giggled as she plastered my dark face with kisses. She sat me down on the dirt floor of our house and admonished my older brothers and sister to take care of me while she went to market to sell her produce.

Stooping, Mom picked up a heavy-laden basket of bananas and balanced it on her head. At age 2, I was unaware of how long Mom was out of the home, only that I felt afraid every time she left the house.

I was too young to realize the dangers Mom faced when she ventured into the overcrowded street markets of Port Au Prince, Haiti.

Our ramshackle home was located in the most violent slum in the northern hemisphere, Cite' Soleil. The streets were overflowing with trash, human and animal feces and homeless people. Those fortunate enough to have a shanty tried to exist quietly so as not to arouse the anger of the more than 30 different gangs that terrorized and controlled the different sectors in the slum.

OUT OF THE SHADOWS

Day after day, Mom left me in the care of my siblings; then one fateful day Mom didn't return home from the market. My father's sister came and took me to her house to live. I was told that Mom had taken sick and died.

I never saw my brothers and sister again. For all I know, they may have been sold as child servants. Though my dad was at times around when Mommy was alive, I never saw him after her death.

My aunt had 12 children of her own, and the shanty she lived in was in a different sector of Cite' Soleil and was much smaller than my family's house had been. The Haitian sun's rays beat down on the metal walls of my new dwelling. By noon, the temperature inside the house was intolerable. I found refuge with some of my cousins under an awning in front of our home.

The dirt road before me had deep potholes one could get lost in. Water mixed with trash ran down in front of our house. It seemed that laundry hung from ropes outside every home. There weren't any yards or grassy areas to play in, so my cousins and I played in the water with the numerous other children that milled around all day.

At night when I lay on my mat on the floor, I could hear the voices of our neighbors as they talked. Not only were the walls of our shanty thin, I could reach out the bedroom window and touch my neighbor's house.

For three years, I lived with my aunt and her family. I slept on the floor sandwiched in between my cousins. Though there were many people around me, I felt alone and frightened. *Where are you, Mommy?* I longed for someone to pick me up the way my mom had when I was a baby and talk softly to me. Many nights I would awaken from a nightmare crying.

"Cry baby, cry baby," my cousins taunted the next morning.

"I'm not," I demanded.

"You should be happy to have a home and not be thrown out on the street with the other garbage."

Shame began to take root in my heart. They were right; at least I had a roof over my head and one or two meals a day.

One morning after a night of horrifying dreams, I heard my aunt call us all to eat. I tried to get up but couldn't. The small room spun in circles. My stomach lurched when I tried to sit up.

My aunt tried to take care of me. She placed cold packs on my feverish chest, encouraged me to drink water and sat by my mat for hours. Realizing that I was not getting better, she took me to the hospital.

Lying in the hospital bed, I was consumed by one thought: *Maybe I'll see you soon, Mommy.* My entire hospital stay was a blur. I knew something was wrong when my aunt stopped coming to see me. When the day came for me to leave the hospital, I didn't go back to the familiar shantytown; rather, I was taken to a small orphanage. There I saw a swarm of children packed into a rectangular room. Benches were pushed to one side as the kids sat and played on the hard stone floor.

"This is your new home," a short dark-skinned woman stated.

"But I don't …"

The lady shoved a rough blanket at me. "This is your bed, go put it in the next room, and change into this uniform."

"Where's my aunt?" I sniffled.

"Go change."

Fear walked with me to the next room. *Why didn't I die, too, Mommy?* I didn't want to change my clothes in front of the other girls who were sitting around and staring at me. I tossed my blanket onto the floor and curled up on top of it.

No one bothered to wake me for supper, and when I finally opened my eyes, darkness greeted me. Suddenly a new urge hit me. I had to use the bathroom but knew I couldn't go out back by myself in the dark. Lying back down, I tried to talk my body out of its need.

My eyes grew accustomed to the darkness, but I still didn't want to go outside to the port-a-potty. I left the sleeping area and headed toward the dining area. My stomach hurt. Tears welled in my eyes from the pain. I snuck into the kitchen and went potty behind the refrigerator. I hated myself for being too afraid to go outside to the restroom. I tiptoed back to my sleeping mat and tried to fall asleep.

In the morning, the dorm mom stood before a trembling group of kids. "Which one of you peed in the kitchen?" she hollered.

REJECTION TO REJOICING

I couldn't raise my head to look her in the eyes when she halted in front of me.

"You!" She grabbed my chin and lifted my face. Her black eyes seemed darker than the midnight sky and more narrowed than a crescent moon. "Well."

Tears streamed down my cheeks. The dorm mom's fingernails pressed firmly into my skin. I closed my eyes. *Mommy, help me.*

"Dismissed," the dorm mom called. I felt the pressure on my face release, only to experience a wrenching pain around my wrist. She dragged me into the kitchen and pushed me to the ground next to the refrigerator. "Clean it up."

The flimsy rag she had thrown at me stunk. The smell of dried urine made my eyes water. After soaking the floor with a soapy solution, I was made to dry the stone floor with the dingy cloth.

I missed breakfast, and by lunch I was starving. A very dark-skinned man plopped a spoonful of beans and mushy bananas on my plate. I stood for a moment with my plate extended toward him.

"That's it. Get moving."

I looked down at my portions and back at him. Suddenly a rough hand pressed down on my shoulders. The dorm mom led me to a bench and plunked me down. The children next to me scooted away. I heard their whispers about being "the potty" girl. My stomach yelled at me to eat, but I was overwhelmed with shame. I dashed from the dining hall to my mat on the floor.

OUT OF THE SHADOWS

I hated the orphanage, the kids, the dorm and myself. *Why did this happen to me? Why doesn't anyone want me?* Rejection took up residence in my heart, along with shame and fear.

For two years, I lived at that orphanage, until one day a new bus came to take many of the children away. Lack of funding forced the orphanage to close. The older children found themselves dumped on the street. The rest of us were divided among the 200 registered orphanages in Haiti.

My new dwelling was an orphanage with high block walls surrounding the complex. A tall black iron gate opened to allow the bus inside the compound. Hordes of children played in the grass and dirt in the open yard.

My old dorm mom led me off the bus. She introduced me to the orphanage's director. I listened to the two adults talk about my history prior to being orphaned.

When we were alone, the director took me onto her lap. My body trembled as she stroked my dirty matted hair. "So you don't have a mommy, huh?"

I shook my head.

"Most of the kids here have lost their parents, or their families can't or don't want to take care of them anymore."

I wanted my body to quit shaking, but I was scared. I couldn't remember the last time anyone had touched me so tenderly. Then an earthquake shook my being as a memory of my mom flashed through my mind. Torrential tears soaked my grimy shirt.

REJECTION TO REJOICING

"Come on, I'll show you around."

There were four long rectangular buildings that made up the compound. One building was where the handicapped children resided. There was a boys' dorm and a girls' dorm, and the final building contained both the lunchroom and the schoolroom.

As the director showed me around, I could feel the stares from the other children. I wanted to find some place to hide. My feet kicked up dirt as I shuffled along. The director reached down and gently took my hand. No one had ever held my hand before. I looked at our entwined fingers and then glanced up at her face. As if seeing her for the first time, I became aware that her pale blue eyes were like the sea, and her white cheeks like the sand on the beach.

She led me toward the girls' dorm. Inside was a long hallway with doors on either side. One huge room was full of metal cribs for the infants; then there was a slightly bigger room with short beds for the toddlers.

"The rooms on this side of the hallway are for the older girls like you. Let's find your bed."

I had never had a bed. I gasped when I walked in and saw the rows of beds stacked on top of each other.

"Here we go," she said, pointing to a bottom bunk farthest from the door. "How's this?"

I nodded at her. I had never seen anything so tidy. The beds all looked the same. Not a single wrinkle. A small lump of a pillow lay at the head of each bed. There were a light blue shirt and a navy jumper lying on my bed.

"This is your uniform," she stated. "After your shower, you can put it on."

"Shower?"

"Yes, once a week the girls take showers. But since you just arrived, and your uniform is clean, you'll need a shower. You can put your old clothes in the waste can."

The director picked up my uniform and led me to the end of the long hallway. Opening the door, I saw a wire rack burdened with white towels. The wall opposite the door had eight showerheads and faucets.

"Well, shower fast, the water doesn't stay warm long," she declared. "Once you're done, come out to the quad where the other children are; we'll be getting ready for dinner soon."

The director left, and the door swung closed. I hated taking off my clothes for fear someone would come in and see me. I ambled forward. *I might as well shower in the street.*

Quicker than a bullet shot from a pistol, I disrobed and showered under a trickle of water. I could hear the squeals of the children outside in the quad playing. I rubbed the towel over my body and dressed in my uniform.

The sun dipped below the tips of the block fence surrounding the compound. Sweat slithered down my back. *What's the point of a shower in this heat?*

The dining hall was silent, even though there were more than 70 kids standing in line to eat. The portions placed on my plate were huge compared to what the other orphanage had to offer.

REJECTION TO REJOICING

In silence, I ate everything on my plate.

After dinner, we went to our dorms for bed. On my bunk was a plain blue t-shirt, five sizes too big. I watched as the older girls put their nightshirts on first, then strategically took off their uniforms. It took some doing, but I copied them. Folding my uniform, I put it at the end of my bed just like everyone else.

The dorm mother came in shortly after we were all in bed. She walked the aisle between the bunks. She stopped by my bed. "Welcome," she said. "In the morning, Gladys will show you how to make your bed properly."

I glanced at the girl on the bottom bunk next to mine. For the first time all day, I received a smile.

Gladys turned out to be a special friend. I don't recall ever having a friend before, and I enjoyed our time together. She was two years older than I was, and so we were in different areas during our time at school. But the rest of the day we were inseparable.

I often would leave my bunk after the other girls were asleep and lie next to Gladys. She was my only comfort and source of joy at the orphanage.

Though I saw the director sometimes, she rarely had contact with any of the children. The dorm moms were in charge of our daily schedule. Some overseers were firm yet kind, while others were strict and never satisfied with anything we did. It was this second group of leaders that would punish everyone for one child's wrongdoings.

One morning during our school lessons, our dorm mom burst into the schoolroom and demanded that all the girls report to the sleeping quarters. I caught up to Gladys in the hall and tried to ask her what was wrong, but her frightened expression halted me.

I mimicked the other girls and stood beside my bed in silence. The dorm mom shoved the door open and stormed down the aisle, two beds away from mine.

"What's the meaning of this?" she hollered.

I noticed the girl the leader was addressing was trembling. "I …"

"Shut up!" the dorm mom screamed. "We put our nightshirts under our pillows when we make our beds."

Producing a black cord from behind her back, the leader demanded the frightened girl turn around. Lash after lash, the cable struck its victim. I couldn't bear the screams. I wanted to run and hide. Then the dorm mom went across the aisle to the other two girls; bunk after bunk, we all received a whipping.

That night, I was huddled next to Gladys before everyone fell asleep. "Why did we all get punished?" I whispered.

"We always do," she replied.

The whippings happened more times than I can remember. Sometimes I tried to hide in the bathroom of the handicapped building. However, when it was discovered that I had not been punished, my lashings were more severe.

My friendship with Gladys was the only ray of light to penetrate my rejected heart. Fear ruled my life day and night. During the day, I was afraid of doing anything wrong. I never wanted the other girls to be punished because of me. At night, I was haunted in my dreams.

One fall day during the second year I was at the second orphanage, a group of foreigners came. They spoke to us through an interpreter about a person named Jesus, who was the Son of God. I had never heard about either person but liked the sound of their strange words and the songs they sang.

During the evening service, one lady came and sat next to me. I didn't know why she sat by me, but I liked hearing her sing. When I glanced up at her, I saw tears in her eyes. I wanted to know if the words of the song had made her cry. Before she left, the lady hugged me.

That night, Gladys and I discussed the missionaries and the words they had said. Neither one of us understood who God was, but we sure liked the hair ribbons, backpacks and books they had brought.

I had enjoyed the visit from the foreigners, but I *really* enjoyed the special attention the kind lady gave to me. Through the interpreter, I learned her name was Debbie, and she was from America.

When the missionaries left, life at the orphanage resumed as normal. I saw my 10th birthday come and go. Gladys once told me if you weren't a baby or toddler, you would never be adopted. Sadness and despair filled my soul and snuffed out any hope I had of ever belonging to a family.

The day after the missionaries left was miserably hot. Our dorm mom ordered us out of the classroom. On our way out to the quad area, the dorm mother handed us each a pile of pebbles.

I tried to keep the small stones from slipping out of my trembling hands. We were made to put the rocks on the ground and then kneel on top of them. The dorm moms yelled at us about leaving lumps in our beds. It seemed like hours that I knelt there, feeling each rock pressing into my skin.

"Please," I whimpered, "I can't take the pain."

"Well, you should stop thinking about yourself and think about the pain you cause us," the dorm mom screamed.

"I want my mommy," I cried.

I hadn't cried for my mommy in years, at least not out loud, but I reasoned I would rather be dead than suffer here at the orphanage.

The dorm mom's cruel laughter pricked me worse than the pebbles I knelt on. When we were finally released, we were told to pick up all our pebbles. Not wanting pressure on my knees, I spent hours bent or squatting to pick up the stones. With the sun's relentless heat scorching my back, I scoured the ground for every rock. Repeatedly, we were called back to pick up more rocks.

Lunch was long past, and my stomach ached. When we finished, we were ushered into our dorm and sent to bed without supper. Gladys and I cried ourselves to sleep.

My body ached as I dressed the next morning. I shuffled behind the other girls toward the dining hall. As I entered the hall, my heart skipped a beat. Debbie and her husband, Dana, were talking to the orphanage's new director, Janet. I was singled out and taken to Janet's office.

"Mary, these people would like to adopt you," Janet stated.

I felt my heart pounding in my chest. *Is this real? Why me?*

"Mary, what do you think about being adopted and going to live in America?"

Words stuck in my throat as if glued. I looked at Debbie and Dana. They were smiling at me, and it seemed their joy spread into their eyes. I would miss Gladys, but to be free from the orphanage was a dream I thought would never come true.

A family in America had also chosen to adopt Gladys. We huddled close together on her bed that night whispering. I never imagined myself leaving Haiti. Joy and fear clashed within my heart. Haiti was my home, my mom's home. Leaving would take me farther away from my mom. Would I forget her? I buried my head in my pillow to muffle my sobs.

Debbie and Dana came to Haiti several times before my adoption was complete. I loved their visits. I had even learned a few words of English to say to them. But each time they left the orphanage without me, I bawled.

The last time Dana came to visit before I left for America, he took me to a salon and asked me if I wanted my cornrows straightened. The solution they used to make my hair straight smelled horrible. My eyes watered from the odor. I think Dana was afraid I was sad to have my hair changed, so I offered him a smile and waved my hand in front of my nose.

I loved how soft and fluffy my hair felt. I had never seen my hair straight and was surprised by how long it really was. The girls in my dorm continuously rubbed my hair. They asked lots of questions about the salon. Even Gladys, who always loved fixing my hair in braids, just stroked my hair, over and over.

Gladys was the first to leave. I stood at the compound gate for hours crying for her. Nighttime was worse. I was alone. I didn't have anyone to sleep next to.

I showered extra long the day Debbie arrived to take me to America. She presented me with a pair of Capri pants and a pretty floral tank top. I felt awkward wearing pants. Boys wore pants, not girls. But Debbie had a pair on, too. I supposed there would be lots about my new home that would be different.

As we waited to board the plane, I noticed Debbie's profile looked strange. Boldly I put my hand on her stomach and nodded. I formed my arms into a cradle and rocked them back and forth. I didn't know how to say "baby" in English, but I hoped she understood. Debbie shrugged her shoulders and offered me a warm smile.

On the airplane ride, I closed my eyes during takeoff and landing. When the plane bounced because of turbulence, I wanted to reach out for Debbie's hand, but fear stopped me.

The trip from the airport to our home in Omaha,

REJECTION TO REJOICING

Nebraska, seemed short. With eyes wider than an owl's, I absorbed the sights around me. The houses seemed so far apart, and the grass in between each home was like a park.

I didn't know much English, but Debbie was talking and pointing to things along the way. What I didn't see were the crowds of people I was accustomed to. There seemed to be more cars than people. In Haiti, there are 843 people per square mile. It seemed you could not stretch out your arms without touching someone. But here in America, there was tons of room, and that frightened me.

However, nothing frightened me more than the huge elephant of a dog that greeted me when I walked into the front door of my new home. Debbie corralled the beast, as I hid behind Dana.

My family walked me around the house, showing me the kitchen, bathroom, their bedroom and finally my room. I couldn't believe there was a room just for me. The house seemed as big as the orphanage's compound.

I crossed the room and looked at a picture of Haitian people hanging on the wall. I turned to Debbie and Dana with tears in my eyes and said, "Thank you."

My parents let me pick the color I wanted my room painted, and I was able to pick out my own bed and bedspread. Though I liked my room, I still hated sleeping alone.

I loved going shopping and seeing people wandering around. I enjoyed playing on the swing in our backyard. And I learned to like our family dog. But the best thing about America was going to church. The music was pretty, and though my English was still very rough, I made friends. The children's pastor and his wife were very kind to me and took time to answer my questions about God and Jesus. The language barrier didn't seem to matter to them. Patiently they shared their faith with me.

Two weeks after my arrival to America, Debbie found out she was pregnant. I had tried to tell them that in the airport, but they had not understood. I was afraid that they might not want me anymore because I had behaved so badly, and because they were going to have their own baby. But Dana and Debbie continued to shower me with their love. Soon I realized they wanted me, and I would forever be a part of their family.

Each day, my English improved; I was starting to understand a lot of things that were said to me. The most dynamic thing I learned was that God wanted to adopt me, too. I couldn't believe that the One who made all things would want anything to do with me. Though I had a new family, I was still the same scared, rejected and ashamed girl.

One night six months after I arrived in America, the most blessed thing happened to me. During children's church, in the basement of Glad Tidings, the children's leader, Maritza, told me Jesus loved me and wanted to adopt me into the family of God. She explained that God had never rejected me, but by sinning, I rejected him. Maritza also told me if I accepted God's forgiveness, he would take away my fears.

REJECTION TO REJOICING

I might not have understood each word Maritza said, but I knew one thing: God loved me. I felt his presence penetrate to the depths of my heart.

What a remarkable night! I knelt in the front row and prayed with Maritza to receive God's forgiveness for my sins and be adopted into his family. I felt like a fish gasping on dry land, and yet, when I started to believe in him, he cast me into the sea of his love. Peace surrounded me like refreshing rain.

I eagerly shared my story with Debbie and Dana when we returned home. They were excited for me and shared some exciting news they had, too. The couple that had adopted Gladys had contacted them online and would be stopping by tomorrow for a visit. Like aloe on sunburn, it seemed God was already working miracles in my life.

The next morning, I sat next to our golden retriever with my nose pressed against the window. I leapt off the couch and darted out the door when I saw an unfamiliar car turn into the driveway.

Gladys and I greeted each other in English, but in our excitement to catch up with each other, we reverted to our mother language. Gladys was happy with her new family, and we spent the day playing with the dog, swinging and laughing.

My faith has become my most treasured possession. God not only was my adopted dad, but my best friend. I don't understand why all these struggles occurred in my life, but in the past years attending church at Eagle's Nest Christian Fellowship, I have learned that God can use my life's trials to help others. God continues to reveal his love for me in many different ways, and it is because of God's love that my heart has been healed. This same love that changed my heart is available to anyone who has given up and lost hope.

When I heard about the earthquake that killed more than 150,000 people near Port Au Prince, Haiti, on January 12, 2010, I wept. My heart ached for the losses each family suffered, and I realized God had spared me by removing me from the country. I hope to return to Haiti someday and share my faith with the many needy people there. Haiti is the poorest nation in the northern hemisphere, but if the people were taught about God and salvation and freedom through Jesus Christ, they would become a wealthy nation.

I still miss my mom, but God has given me two wonderful families, the Goodwaters and my eternal heavenly family. I am forever rejoicing in my position as adopted daughter of the King of Kings.

REFLECTIONS
The Story of Callie
Written by Karen Koczwara

"You look like a skeleton." My roommate stood me in front of the full-length mirror, her face etched with worry. "Your bones are sticking out everywhere, Callie. You are a sick girl."

I shook my head vehemently, fighting back angry tears. "I'm not, I'm not," I argued. The girl staring back at me was no skeleton. In fact, if I could be honest, she still needed to lose a couple more pounds. I was *not* sick.

"Callie, please. Take a good look at yourself," my friend begged. "You need help."

I forced myself to look again in the mirror. I didn't see the gaunt, pale face, the protruding cheekbones, the hollow eyes. I was just your average everyday college student, minus the "freshmen 15" everyone fretted about. So what if I lived off lettuce pieces — who cared? At least I wasn't spilling out of my jeans like some of the girls around campus!

"I'm just trying to be a friend," my roommate sighed, stepping away from the mirror. "I care about you, Callie, and so do a lot of people."

I only half heard her last words. I was already calculating the steps I'd need to run tonight after everyone had gone to bed to make up for eating too much. If I could finish my studying, I could slip out and run the stairs for an hour or two. Maybe sneak in a few sit-ups, too, if I wasn't too tired.

Suddenly self-conscious, I yanked a sweatshirt over my head and grabbed my backpack for class. As I stood to my feet, I grew dizzy. I was getting dizzy pretty often these days. Must be freshman stress, I concluded as I slammed the door behind me. Yes, that must be it.

~~~

Little girls have a lot to worry about. There is the issue of which doll to play with, what dress to wear Sunday morning, which friend to hopscotch with at recess, what flavor of ice cream to pick at the county fair.

Growing up, I worried about all those things. But starting at a young age, something else weighed on my mind. I had a terrible secret, one I feared I could never, ever tell anyone.

When I was growing up near Seattle, Washington, my family consisted of two loving parents, an older brother, Nick, another brother and a younger sister, Lisa. My parents were both prominent members of the Lutheran church; from the outside, we were the average American family living the dream. But when I was 4 years old, my nightmare began.

"Come here, Callie. Let's go look at the chickens," my grandfather said one afternoon. He took my hand and dragged me out back toward the chicken coop. I followed obediently.

REFLECTIONS

"Here, chickies!" I called out, racing happily through the coop. I loved being outdoors more than anything.

"Callie." My grandfather grabbed my hand again and pulled me aside. His voice grew stern as he looked me in the eye. "Grandpa wants to show you something, okay?" He exposed himself to me and wanted me to touch him.

I flinched. Something about this didn't seem right. I glanced around, but no one else was in sight. Nervously, I did what my Grandpa wanted me to do. A yucky feeling ran through me as I yanked my hand back.

My grandpa smiled, but it wasn't a pleasant smile. "Now, this is going to be our little secret, okay? You never tell anyone about this, ever, you hear me? I'll hurt you if you do."

I nodded, feeling sick inside. I wanted to run back to the chickens, but Grandpa wasn't finished yet.

"Tell Grandpa, do you sometimes do things with your brothers? Touch them like you touched me?"

I shook my head back and forth. "No!" I cried.

"Are you sure?" he pressed. "I'm surprised you haven't seen their private parts."

"I haven't!" I repeated, growing upset. Why was Grandpa asking me all these questions? I didn't like this one bit! I'd always been a bit scared of Grandpa. More than once, he gave me an apple and made me eat the whole thing, core and all. He seemed to like it when I gagged on the last few bits. Another time, he offered me candy from the candy drawer but then told me I had to "earn" it. Most kids I knew didn't have to earn candy from their grandparents' candy drawer. Today, I disliked Grandpa even more. But I would keep my promise and never tell anyone because I didn't want him to hurt me.

One night, my brother Nick slipped into my room as I was falling asleep and climbed into bed with me. He grabbed my hand and told me to touch him. I cringed. I could see Grandpa's face, twisted into a sick smile as he said the same words. Why was this happening to me? I was a good little girl!

Nick insisted, threatening to get me in trouble if I did not do what he said. So I did what he wanted, my stomach churning the whole time. I just wanted to go back to playing with dolls and swinging on the playground. Why couldn't everyone just leave me alone?

My grandpa died two years later, and a wave of relief flooded me. He had made me touch him several more times, and I was happy he would never be able to do this again. With him gone, I was able to work up the guts to tell my mother what had happened.

"Oh, honey! I'm so sorry! That's terrible!" My mother pulled me in for a hug. "Why didn't you say something sooner, you poor thing?"

"Grandpa made me promise to not tell. He said he would hurt me," I replied in a small voice.

"Well, he will never hurt you again," my mother replied quietly.

Nick continued his inappropriate behavior. When I was 9 years old, I finally told my parents the awful truth. I expected them to be filled with rage, perhaps even kick him out of the house. While my mother was horrified, my father kept his cool. "We will take care of this," he assured me. "Nick will never do that to you again."

I wanted to believe this was true, but two people I'd thought I could trust had already harmed me. Who would be next?

Life went on. My parents continued their involvement with the church; they were prominent members of the community, respected by all. Each Sunday, we plastered smiles to our faces, put on our best clothes and sat in the pews with the other smiling families. I sang along to the songs and half-listened to the Bible stories about a God who loved us. Inside, however, my heart could not connect this love to my life. If God was so good, why had he let my grandpa and brother do this to me?

When I reached junior high, I kept up my goody-two-shoes image, trying to do right by everyone. I wanted to please the world; if I could just keep the smile on my face, no one would be able to see the pain beneath.

In high school, I got involved with a group called Young Life. I began studying my Bible on a regular basis and attending outings with my peers. My sophomore year, I joined a small discipleship group with seven other kids. We all kept each other accountable and shared our most intimate thoughts. I, of course, kept much of my pain stuffed inside; it was safer that way.

In June that year, we planned a hiking trip to Canada. I was excited about the opportunity to spend more time with my new friends. We would have plenty of time to study the Bible together, as well as explore the outdoors. I never could have imagined the turn this trip would take.

One day, after we had been hiking for a number of hours, a huge snowstorm blew in out of nowhere. As the flakes pelted our faces and the temperature began to drop, one of our leaders began to show signs of hypothermia; she had to be flown out by emergency helicopter. When one of the young people began to show signs of this, too, the leaders began to worry. "We'd better all get in our tents and huddle together," they suggested. "We've got to stay warm and ride this thing out."

We all tried to stay calm as we pitched our tents and climbed inside. The wind whipped at our thin vinyl shelter as we wrapped ourselves in our sleeping bags. One of my leaders, a man in his early 30s, scooted behind me and slipped his arms around my back. "I'll keep you warm," he whispered in my ear.

I didn't like the feel of this. He was a married man with two small children. He was also my history teacher and soccer coach. Was he hitting on me? I tried to play innocent and ignore him, but before I knew what was happening, he moved in for a kiss. "C'mon, you know you like it," he hissed, pressing his lips against mine.

"What are you doing?" I whispered back, trying to pull away. He only pressed harder, and I began to feel sick. My grandpa, Nick and now my youth leader! Was it me? Was I the one asking for it? What was wrong with me to be attracting this unwanted attention?

I spent the rest of the trip in a daze. When we arrived

back home, my leader tried to contact me. "I really need to talk to you, Callie," he begged. "I know it's crazy, but I really like you, and I want to see you again. Please, don't let me down."

"You're sick," I replied, my voice thick with disgust. "You're a married man!" I slammed down the phone and prayed I'd never see him again.

In a way, I was relieved to graduate high school. I had enjoyed Young Life and the new friends I'd made, but it would be nice to start fresh away at college. I left home and headed to Pacific Lutheran University to begin my freshman year. I was a bit nervous when I arrived. I'd always been shy, but thanks to playing sports in high school, I'd met lots of friends. Right away I tried out for choir, as I had always had a passion for singing, and I figured it would be a great way to meet new people.

Like most kids away at college their first year, I gained a few pounds. One day, my roommate commented on my appearance. "Looks like you're enjoying that cafeteria pizza a little too much," she teased, nodding at my stomach. "'Freshmen 15,' eh?"

I glanced down at my jeans, which were indeed growing a little snug. Horrified that I'd packed on the pounds in such a short amount of time, I vowed right then and there to do something about it. I began cutting things out of my diet right and left, until I was left eating nothing more than a lettuce leaf a day. The weight flew off; before long, I was thinner than I'd ever been. When I wasn't studying or attending class, I exercised as much as I could.

Once the lights went out in our dorm, I snuck out of my room and ran up and down the stairs. When I returned to my bed, I did several dozen sit-ups. I refused to ever be called fat again.

When my roommate stood me in front of the mirror that day and reported I looked like a skeleton, I denied it. The girl staring back at me was far from skinny; in fact, she could probably lose a bit more weight. I tried to keep focused on my studies, but I grew so weak and tired that I had to drop out of my early morning class. It was hard to focus throughout the day, but I continued to watch every bite that went into my mouth.

One day, my mother called, her voice full of concern. "I was watching TV this morning, and this documentary came on. It was about a girl who suffered from anorexia. It's an eating disorder, Callie, and I think you might have it." She paused. "I really want you to come home so we can get you help."

When spring semester was over, I returned home and agreed to go to a psychologist, hoping to appease my mother. "You definitely have an eating disorder," the doctor confirmed. "I want you to begin eating all of your meals in front of your parents. This will help you stay accountable. It is very vital to your healing process." He pulled out a prescription pad. "I also want you to start taking Prozac for depression."

To further cloud matters, my relationship with my high-school sweetheart, Scott, was rocky. We had gotten engaged, but as I became more and more distant and troubled, Scott began to back away. I loved Scott and had given my virginity away to him. I felt guilty about this, as I'd held on for so long, trying to do the morally right thing. Doing the right thing was starting to feel futile, however. Depressed and confused, I broke off the engagement with Scott that fall.

I continued to feel defeated. Deep down, I knew that food wasn't the true source of my issues. I sat across from my parents night after night, slowly chewing my food. I felt sick afterward, though, mad at myself for eating so much. I had to get it off my body right now!

One evening, after my mother insisted I finish my dinner, I fled down the hall and threw it all up. It felt good to vomit — and suddenly, a light bulb went on. If I could just throw up my food, I could eat whatever I wanted without guilt! Why hadn't I thought of this before?

I began bingeing and purging from that moment on. Consumed with food, I started keeping my eyes out for "deals" wherever I went.

I soon learned that one hamburger joint had 40-cent cheeseburgers on Wednesdays; I'd order 10 of them and wash them down with a large Diet Coke. Sometimes I'd buy a whole pizza on sale and sit in the parking lot, devouring it all in one sitting.

Another time, I ordered a whole cake from a bakery and shoved it all in my mouth within minutes. As soon as I got home, I threw it all up, relief washing over me as I flushed the toilet. I would often stay up all night, eating and puking, until I either ran out of food or fell asleep from sheer exhaustion. Then the cycle would continue the next day.

I had gotten a job at a local restaurant as a waitress. To maintain my bingeing habit, I discovered a little trick. If I took the carbon copy of a patron's order to the cooks, I could get them to re-make the meal. I'd then take the plate of pancakes or sandwich into the back room and scarf it down. I was so consumed with food that I didn't stop to realize I was stealing from my employer.

"I thought we just made that order," one of the cooks barked one day, scratching his head as he held up the carbon copy I'd handed him.

"Nope, you didn't. It's a busy day; I know it's hard to keep track," I replied, laughing nervously.

When I quit my job, my employer threw me a party. "We don't know what we'll do without you. We'll miss you," my boss declared, raising his glass in the air. "Cheers to Callie!"

My face grew hot; I felt terrible for the way I'd deceived everyone. I didn't deserve a party; I deserved to be fired. Tears filled my eyes abruptly as everyone walked up to pat my back. I was the worst person in the world.

"God, what am I doing?" I cried when I got home that night. I threw myself on my bed and began to sob. To ease my sorrows, I pulled the box of a dozen donuts out from under my bed and shoved them in my mouth. Soon, there were only crumbs left.

That summer, I began seeing a Christian psychologist. Several people had highly recommended him, and I was hopeful that he would be able to pinpoint the root of my eating disorder and help me.

Initially, Dr. Berkman seemed like the answer to my prayers. But after a few sessions, I began to grow uneasy in his office. One day at the end of our time, he stepped out from behind his desk, walked over and pulled me in for a long hug. Then, in a shocking move, he planted a kiss on my mouth. "You're such a pretty girl, Callie," he whispered in my ear. "So sweet, too. Such a lovely girl."

I was so taken aback I didn't know what to say. I'd just bared my soul to this man, assuming he was a professional, and now he was making the moves on me. Grandpa, Nick, my youth leader — it was all too familiar. I pulled myself back and stared at the ground in shame. "I … I'd better go," I stammered, running out the door.

I continued to see Dr. Berkman and actually found myself enjoying the attention. Though I had been dating a man quite seriously, I realized a part of me was always longing for extra affection. One day, Dr. Berkman confessed to me, "If I could be with you, Callie, I would in a heartbeat. My wife is out of town this week. Why don't you come over to my house tomorrow night? Just once. You won't regret it."

Again, I found myself speechless. Dr. Berkman was a married man with two of his own children. He was also the leader of a major Christian organization. To the world, he was a highly regarded religious man. While the attention was flattering, I knew deep down this was terribly wrong. Dr. Berkman was way out of line.

One afternoon, my brother and sister-in-law happened to be visiting the same office building when they saw me preparing to go into Dr. Berkman's office. They took me out for coffee at a restaurant down the street, and I confessed what my doctor had been doing with me. My brother was horrified.

"You have to stop seeing this guy right away! Do you know how wrong that is?" he cried. I knew deep down, but there was a battle raging within me whether I should keep seeing Dr. Berkman professionally or not. He had tried to convince me that it was okay, but I wanted to tell him that I was not coming back.

"I know, I know …" I began, too flustered to sort out my words. Why did it seem like trouble found me wherever I went?

I phoned from the restaurant to cancel my appointment. Dr. Berkman quizzed me over the phone. "Where are you?" When I told him, he immediately came down to the restaurant to talk to me.

My brother approached Dr. Berkman with strong words. "You leave my sister alone, you hear me? There's no way you can remain in a professional relationship with her after what you have done."

"I'm sorry," Dr. Berkman replied hastily. "I really never saw this coming. I've never had this happen to me before, but your sister, well, she's really something special."

"Yes, she is special. So keep your hands off!" my brother retorted.

REFLECTIONS

I later discovered that the doctor's claim of never having done this before was a lie. I chose to stop seeing him at that time, but the experience with Dr. Berkman sent me over the edge. I began drinking to ease my pain. I'd spent so many years trying to do the right thing, be a good girl, but now it all seemed pointless. I couldn't seem to find the right path, no matter which way I turned. Alcohol seemed like the easiest answer.

A few drinks turned into many more. After work, I headed to the nearest bar, where I sat for hours as the bartender poured me one after another. I hardly recognized the girl I'd become, the girl who had once studied the Bible for hours with youth group, memorizing verse after verse. I'd been so desperate to know God in a tangible manner, but life's circumstances always seemed to stand in the way. I feared I'd never find my path back to him again.

I started dating again and began sleeping around. The one-night stands meant nothing to me; I didn't care if men hurt me or if I hurt them. My heart was calloused and growing numb. Beneath it all, I was desperate to feel loved but no longer believed I deserved it.

One night I met a Navy pilot in a bar and began dating him. Two months later, I missed my period. Panic set in as I tried to recall the last time I'd had sex. Within a few days, I learned I was pregnant. I told my boyfriend, and he suggested I get an abortion.

"You're too young to lose your freedom," he told me. "Just get rid of it."

I made an appointment the next day. The procedure was painful, but it hardly matched the pain that seared my heart.

My reckless behavior went on. I continued to drink and began shoplifting, something I'd sworn I'd never do. One day, I sauntered into a store and walked out with some coloring books and pens. I had absolutely no use for them and no idea why I'd done it, but nevertheless, I got caught.

"You really don't seem like the type to do something like this and definitely not the type to go to jail," the officer at the police station told me. "We're going to put you on probation, but if this happens again, you're going to have to serve time, okay?" He seemed almost sympathetic as he wrote up my report.

I hung my head, tears of humiliation stinging my eyes. I couldn't believe I'd stooped this low. Inside, I was screaming at the top of my lungs, wanting desperately to be heard, loved and understood. I'd hit another new low, and this time, climbing out of that hole seemed virtually impossible.

"I heard about something I think would be really helpful for you," my mom told me one day. "There's this modeling school in town that my friend takes her daughter to. It might be really good for your self-esteem. Why don't you give it a try?"

At first, I rolled my eyes. Modeling school? That seemed a bit farfetched. I reluctantly agreed to sign up. I entered a beauty pageant a few months later. I'd always loved singing at church; I felt that singing was my way of expressing what was on the inside. My voice teacher encouraged me to sing a solo for the talent portion of the pageant, and I managed to win the runner-up position. While the experience was fun, the overall environment was toxic for me. The extreme pressure to be beautiful and perfect on the outside was simply too much. My insides were still an ugly mess, and until I dealt with them, it didn't matter how many beautiful dresses I donned or what I did with my hair.

I went to live in the trailer on my Nonnie's property after this. Nonnie was my maternal grandmother and had been a wonderful influence my whole life. She sat me down one day for a long talk. "Child, I know life can be hard. Lord knows I made many mistakes growing up. But God is so good, and he has delivered me from my past. His mercy is new every morning. Just cling to him, and he will give you the answers."

I was so thankful for the opportunity to spend time with Nonnie. I felt she was one of the few people who truly cared for me and saw through to my heart. I wanted to believe what she said, that God's mercies were new every day. Yet, were they for me, the girl who might have pushed it one too many times? Could God really restore my heart?

Soon after this, I landed a job at a brokerage firm in Seattle. I was elated, as it was an opportunity that could turn into a potentially lucrative career. I began dating a guy named Steve; he was kind and seemed to genuinely care for me. But my drinking, depression and eating disorder took a toll on our relationship, and shortly after we got engaged, he broke up with me.

I began seeing another psychologist, this time a woman named Kerry Lawson who was herself a recovered anorexic. She was helpful in some ways, but I continued to hold onto the deep-rooted pain in my life.

A few years later, I lost my job at the brokerage firm after they went bankrupt following the Black Monday stock market crash in 1987. This was yet another blow. But two months later, I received a much larger blow when my father's double life was exposed.

My father's sister had been going to counseling for some time, trying to deal with the pain of her own past. Eventually, the horrible truth came out. My grandfather, who had sexually abused me, had also abused his own children. My dad had carried this terrible secret with him all his life and continued the cycle with his own destructive choices, including maintaining a sexual relationship with his own sister. While he'd remained a faithful husband and father on the outside, he'd spent his entire existence living a double life.

As we lived in a rural town 40 minutes outside of Seattle, my father was forced to commute into work every day. He was never late coming home for dinner; in fact, he would often stop off at the farmers' market on his way home for fresh vegetables and still never arrive home late. But as it turned out, he'd been going to strip clubs and hiring prostitutes during the daytime. He claimed he never had sex with them, that he "drew the line" at that. Nevertheless, my mother was devastated.

"I had no idea, no idea," she sobbed, unable to get off the couch for weeks. "I thought we were this perfect Christian family, you know? I love my job; I love my kids, my husband …" Her voice trailed off as she buried her face in her hands. She sank into a deep depression, and for the next few months, she began drinking heavily for the first time in her life, trying to ease her own pain.

My heart felt sick. My father, though sometimes critical, had always been a strong presence in my life. He'd never missed a sporting event and was always looking for ways to spend time with us kids. I never would have dreamed that he would destroy our trust by doing such a thing. Once again, the destructive cycle continued, leaving more hurting hearts in its wake.

With a drinking problem and no job, my choice of living situations was limited. I moved in with my sister and her family, but she told me I needed to get my act together or leave. She began intercepting phone calls for me at all hours of the night from men she didn't know — and I barely knew myself.

Eventually, my sister kicked me out of her house. I didn't blame her; she had her own family to protect. I called up my parents, hoping I could stay there until I could get back on my feet. They allowed me to move home, under certain conditions.

I went to AA classes, but they didn't help much. I knew I was headed nowhere fast, but the pain seemed too thick to try to wade through. That's when they told me I had to leave.

"I'm sorry, Callie. It's not okay for you to live here and continue to drink," my mother insisted. She and my father had begun counseling, but they still had a long road of healing ahead of them.

Desperate, I called up my brother Nick. He was a last resort, but I was on the verge of homelessness. He was a tugboat captain, working two weeks on, one week off. He was now married to his third wife, who was an alcoholic like me.

"Sure, you can come crash here," Nick agreed. "Anything for my little sis."

I felt sick at his words. I was hoping Nick had changed; I could put the past behind us if he could.

One night during his week off, Nick suggested we all go out drinking. It sounded like a good plan to me. We took separate cars to the bar downtown, where I ordered one drink after another, trying to drown my sorrows. Nick headed home first in his vehicle, and I said I'd be home shortly. At last, the bartender shook his head. "No more, lady. You need to call a cab and get home."

The next thing I knew, I woke up to Nick's wife dressing me in a pair of pajamas on the couch. "C'mon, honey, just put your legs in, okay?" she crooned, gently nudging me.

I rubbed my eyes. "Where am I, and what happened?" I mumbled groggily.

"You passed out, sweetie. You tried to drive home and

had a little accident. But it's all good now. Just go back to sleep."

My head was throbbing, my mind was spinning. I'd just done what? I racked my brain, trying to remember the last few hours. I'd been talking to the bartender, and then … surely, I hadn't tried to drive home? What on earth was wrong with me?!

I was almost asleep when, to my horror, Nick crawled into the living room on all fours. He was stark naked. "Hey, Sis," he murmured, inching toward me.

"What are you doing?" I cried. I was disgusted: The same guy who had hurt me as a child was back again; he hadn't changed a bit. Too woozy to move, I closed my eyes and blacked out.

The next morning, I began freaking out. Surely, I hadn't done anything with Nick, had I?

"Don't you remember last night? It was a good time," Nick hissed in my ear, chuckling.

I felt sick at his laugh. No, no, this wasn't happening. I had to get out of here, figure out what had happened to my car and never come back!

I called my mother, who had already begun to piece things together. "Callie, a lady from our church called this morning. They found your car 20 minutes from here. What in the world is going on?"

"I can explain," I cried. "I just need to come home."

My brother drove me home. I was too disgusted to look at him. The image from last night was burned into my memory forever. I slammed the door of his car and tried not to look back as he sped away. I hoped I would never see him again.

"We're very upset about this, Callie," my mother said sadly, sitting me down. "You are a 26-year-old woman. You need to start making better choices in your life, or you are going to end up dead. Do you hear what I'm saying?"

I nodded somberly. I wanted so badly to explain that I *did* want to make good choices, that I'd been trying to do just that since I was a little girl, but the bad things always seemed to find me first. I'd never meant to hurt anyone, myself included. I was at the end of my rope and needed help fast.

I agreed to enter rehab for 30 days. There, in the quiet of my room, I cried out to God, asking him to please free me of my addictions and help me get on the right path. I wasn't sure he still heard me, as I'd spent so long living a destructive life. The girl in church youth camp was only a distant memory, a stranger I might not recognize if we passed each other on the street.

As I cried out to God, I felt a peace come over me. It was unlike anything I'd ever known. I'd tried so hard to figure things out on my own, but each time I thought I'd made progress, I found myself right back at the start. I'd feared the rest of my life would be a two-steps-forward, three-steps-backward process. I'd all but given up on being whole again. But as I lay there in my bed staring up at the ceiling, I felt God ask me if I could truly rely on him. He seemed to be asking me if I could move my dependence on alcohol and food to him. He would be my all, if I would just surrender it all.

All the memories of my childhood came flooding back: my grandpa's behavior, the other men in my life, my abortion, the drunken nights, the bingeing and purging, the stealing. I remembered Nonnie's words: "His mercies are new every day." For the first time, I was able to believe that his mercy was intended for me. God did not play games; there was nothing I could do or say to make him love me any more or less. He just loved me, plain and simple. At last, I could accept that love for myself! What a wonderful feeling of freedom.

While in a small group meeting in rehab, I met a man named Brad. He was battling a drug and alcohol addiction of his own. We began confiding in each other, sharing stories and triumphs as we got through each day. I found myself attracted to Brad's kindness, and when we got out, we began talking on the phone. After I flew up to his hometown in Alaska, we began dating more seriously. That winter, just a few weeks before Christmas, Brad and I got married.

I moved with Brad to the small town of Seward, Alaska, where he was a commercial fisherman. Coming from the city of Seattle, I found it quite an adjustment settling into life in a town of 3,000 people. I enjoyed the rugged scenery, though, and found most of the locals to be especially friendly. For the first time in years, I began to feel free. Miraculously, while I was in rehab, God had taken away my desire to drink and binge.

Brad's father, who owned a retail store in Seward, had passed away earlier that year. It became too much for his mother, who worked full time as a registered nurse, to run on her own. So Brad sold his boat and all his commercial fishing gear, and we began operating the store together. I now had a fresh start in my new town.

Shortly after moving to Seward, we learned my beloved Nonnie had passed away. I was devastated. Nonnie had been one of the biggest positive influences in my life, always encouraging me to hold on to God and receive his love. At her funeral, I saw my brother Nick, and the memories of that night came flooding back. I wasn't sure I would ever be able to forgive him in my heart.

On February 5, 1994, I gave birth to our firstborn, a son named Jake. Two years later, our daughter, Samantha, was born. Brad and I were thrilled to be parents.

One day, while working at the store, I happened to step outside and see a familiar figure across the street. Straining my eyes, I gasped as I realized who it was. My brother Nick, the one who had caused me so much shame, was literally feet away from me! Taking a deep breath, I walked across the street and gave him a big hug.

"What are you doing here?" I asked.

"The tugboat I was running broke down outside the bay. We're gonna have to stay here until it's fixed." He spoke nonchalantly, as though we saw each other every day, as though a world of pain had not separated us the past few years.

I took another deep breath. "Well, Nick, I have to get

back inside, but I just want you to know something. I love you." I couldn't believe I'd uttered those words. They had truly come from God, as in my own flesh I could not have said them.

Nick grew quiet. "Take care, Callie," he said, smiling. And that was that.

❧❧❧

Brad and I became involved in our church, Eagle's Nest Christian Fellowship. We loved the intimate atmosphere, kind people and caring pastors.

When Debbie and Dana Goodwater came onboard, we were more than thrilled. Debbie and Dana have a special vision for the church and its people and truly care about each person. Over the past few years, they have invested their hearts in each of us, encouraging us to grow closer to God.

One day Debbie casually suggested, "Callie, have you ever thought about going off the antidepressant medicine?"

My response was, "Whoa! Now that's a concept I had long ago dismissed!" I had taken Prozac for more than 20 years and had tried many times to stop, only to sink to a new low I could not pull myself out of. I had no idea how I would function without it.

But as I took this to God in prayer, I heard him gently reply to me, "I am more than enough for you." And with God's help, I was able to stop altogether and never go back. I no longer need the pills because my God sustains me completely.

As I chose to seek him first above all things, my worries about family and life began to fall into perspective — God's perspective. He truly does add *all* things to me — my children, husband, work — when he is my focus.

There was still more to be healed in my heart. One night, as I was praying, God began to show me that my abortion had broken his heart. I saw him holding that baby in his hands, keeping it safe. He then showed me that I was forgiven, that I could release this painful act once and for all. As I wept for my unborn child, I thanked God for his mercies, new every day. He had restored my life, blessing me with two wonderful children. My cup overflowed!

I have always loved music, especially singing. Not long ago, I began playing the piano at church and leading worship. As I ran my fingers over the ivory keys, I gave thanks to the Lord for restoring my life. Never in a million years had I believed that I, with my destructive past, would be able to sit before my church and praise God. I have discovered that it is in the place of worship, adoring the One who is worthy, that healing comes — and boy, does it feel good!

Just the other day, I happened to catch my reflection in the mirror. Staring back was a woman who made me smile. Her eyes lit up, her smile sparkled, her face was flushed with passion for life. I couldn't help but recall the person in the mirror all those years ago. I was a wisp of a girl, wasting away outside and inside. I'd tried to stuff away the pain, but only God had been able to set me free. Now, my reflection makes me smile. Because I see someone else in that mirror: I see Jesus. And I'm pretty sure he's smiling, too.

THE CANARY SINGS
The Story of Pam Collman
Written by Marty Minchin

"Hey, Pam," Dean, a boy from school I hardly know, calls out to me one gorgeous, sunny California afternoon. "You want to ride my motorcycle after school today?"

Tenth grade isn't that interesting to me, nor are most 10th-grade boys. However, I won't turn away a boy with a motorcycle. I am fearless, and if anything seems even remotely dangerous, I'm there.

"Sure," I reply, my cool voice disguising my growing excitement. "There's a big dirt field behind my house. I'll meet you there after classes."

After school, Dean roars up on a Husky 250, a sleek ride that looks as if it can easily handle the soft dirt. I follow him out to the open field, and I feel my adrenaline pump as Dean hands me a helmet. I snap it on and confidently take the bike from him. It is heavier than I thought; I am only 100 pounds, and I know this bike well outweighs me.

I climb on and kick off, and the roar of the bike's motor feels amazing. The bike handles easily as I head straight out into the field, bright with afternoon light, giving it a little gas as my confidence grows. This is easy.

The wheels spin a bit as the bike hits a mini sand dune, but I press the machine forward and rev it to power it up the hill. The front wheel gives a little as it bites into the deep sand, turning and kicking up the grit against my legs. I shift my body to straighten it out, but I don't weigh enough to balance the bike. Gravity takes over. All I can think about is the searing hot exhaust pipe inches from my calf.

If I don't get off this bike now, it's going to fall on me, and I'll get burned.

The bike starts to lean, and I fling myself off it, hoping to clear the bike. I brace for a hard landing, but instead I hit a moving surface. My body bounces off the back wheel, then thumps into the gritty ground. The blue summer sky fills my vision, and the screaming of the motorcycle's engine, which is still going full throttle while the bike lies on its side, floods my ears.

"My leg!" I scream, my voice no competition for the motorcycle's wailing. "My leg is stuck in the wheel!"

Dean doesn't hear my frantic yelling over the relentless shrieks of the motorcycle, and he can't see me on the ground.

I grab my leg, which is stuck in the revolving back wheel, and hold on to it with every bit of strength I have. If I let go, the wheel will rip my whole leg off.

Time slows as I call on all of my strength to pull my leg toward me, away from the certain mutilation the spinning wheel promises. *Please, someone help me.* I can't twist myself around to see how much of my leg is trapped, so I can only imagine the worst.

It's gone. My leg is gone.

THE CANARY SINGS

ﾝﾝﾝ

Dean sprints toward me and turns off the bike, mercifully silencing the machine's noisy agony. He extracts my leg from the wheel, hoists me up like a broken doll and carries me the eighth-mile to my garage. Blood is dripping from my leg, leaving a dark trail in the dirt behind us.

I can't see that my pants are still on, covering my leg that's still there. I don't know what's happened, but I know that my foot had been in that bike wheel. I can't feel anything, but I'm so frightened that I keep screaming, anyway.

Neighbors rush over to help, and people hold my leg up to slow the bleeding while we wait for the ambulance. Their concerned faces lean over me, but I'm not listening to what they say.

"My leg is gone!" I continue to bellow, cussing and cursing God out loud, even though my leg, which people are hoisting in the air, is right in front of my eyes. The garage is covered with blood, like a crime scene.

"You stop that," my mom hisses in my ear. "God did not do this to you."

ﾝﾝﾝ

When I'm settled in the hospital, I learn that the wheel of the motorcycle severed a good portion of my heel off. Apparently I was screaming from pure panic, because the nerves had been cut, and I couldn't feel the pain.

OUT OF THE SHADOWS

My dad, the administrator at this hospital in Santa Maria, walks into my room to break some bad news.

"Pam, the doctors don't think you're going to walk again. You've lost a lot of your heel bone and a lot of the skin off the bottom of your foot. They're considering amputating your foot." He looks at me sadly, stern and official in his business suit.

"No, no," I tell him, my voice strong. I am a determined and stubborn girl, and I refuse to take any declaration from doctors, or my dad for that matter, as truth. I may be stuck in a bed right now, but this is not permanent. "I'm going to walk. Watch me."

A few days later, my mom's friend Juanita steps in the door. She is beautiful, with long black hair and high cheekbones. She exudes a motherly, spiritual air, and I recognize her as the confidante who listens as my mom pours out her troubles with my dad and me. Juanita prays with Mom, and they pray for me.

"God showed me your heart the day of the accident," Juanita tells me in her smooth, soothing voice. "God showed me that you are a little canary bird that he loves and wants to protect. You keep wanting to be like the wild birds, but God wants to protect you. You were created to sing to him."

She carefully straightens my sheets, smiling her beautiful wide smile, and I think about what she has told me. I have no doubt that Juanita has revealed the Spirit of God.

"He's not going to leave you alone, Pam."

THE CANARY SINGS

God, I know you love me so much that you saved me from my rebellious ways. But I'm not ready to follow you right now.

ॐॐॐ

I have been a chronic runner, a bolter. On several occasions, I have set off down the highway, walking along the lonely shoulder and feeling the breeze from the passing cars. Sometimes I stop and motion for some driver to pick me up and take me anywhere that's away from my parents and this town. Every time, I come back home on my own accord — except one time.

My parents fight and argue all of the time, threatening each other with divorce almost every day. Mom has left Dad a few times, but she always comes back. My parents frequently take out their anger on me, physically and emotionally. Plus, my mom and I have been at odds as long as I can remember. Running seems like a good solution to problems too overwhelming to solve.

By the time I am a young teenager, I have no self-worth, and I think I am here to be used and abused. I have taken up smoking marijuana and sleeping around, and at age 14, I finally run away and stay away. Police later find me wandering the streets of San Francisco, drugged and trying to escape the company of pimps and prostitutes.

The police bring me home, but things don't get better. Mom just becomes more vigilant in talking about God and following me around the house.

The day before the motorcycle crash, I have had enough of Mom's God talk. I stride into my bedroom and shut the door to block out her voice.

God, would you just leave me alone? I can't take this anymore.

All I hear is silence.

తతత

One bright spot in my life has been my grandparents, who are beautiful, godly people. They are the only people I know who show that God loves people unconditionally. When Mom and Dad get into their bigger fights, Mom takes us to live in Texas for a few months with my grandparents, who take us to church.

One Sunday, the preacher delivers a fiery sermon imploring us to get saved so we won't go to hell. He waves his arms like a conductor, his voice rising and falling as he describes the horrors that await unsaved souls.

I am 12, and the thought of going to hell frightens me to my core. I don't have the maturity to understand grace and love, but I understand fear. I ask Jesus to save me on the spot.

A year later, we are back in Texas, and I hear another rousing sermon, this one on how we'd better be ready because Jesus could come back at any time. I hear the urgency in the preacher's voice, especially when he describes the rapture.

That evening, I sit on the balcony outside my bedroom

and think about the preacher's words.

I stay up the whole night staring at the bright stars set against their black canvas, my mind sharp in the crisp night air. For hours, I beg God to split the sky open, and get the rapture started.

Come tonight and get me, God. I'm clean, I'm forgiven and I'm ready for you right now. I can't stay good much longer. There's no way I'll be good my whole life.

The sky doesn't change, other than the stars and moon making their nightly revolutions across the heavens. As the rising sun lightens the horizon, I'm still sitting here on earth, on this little balcony.

෴෴෴

The motorcycle crash halts my young teenage rebellion.

Suddenly, I am bedridden. When I am moved home, I take up residence in a hospital bed in my bedroom. Over the next two years, I have a series of reconstructive surgeries on my foot, and each recovery requires months of lying on my back with my foot elevated higher than my heart. I can't go outside because I have so little skin on the bottom of my foot that I'm at a high risk for infection.

Even if I want to, there is literally no way I can go outside to smoke pot, run away, drink or have sex. The scars from surgeries moving skin from other parts of my body to my foot take away any desire I have to wear a bikini, a former staple of my wardrobe.

OUT OF THE SHADOWS

This canary's wings have been clipped.

The days are long, and I have a lot of time to pass. I read, do crossword puzzles and learn how to needlepoint. Sometimes my friends stop by for a visit, but I am otherwise cut off from teenage social life. I once get up on crutches well enough to go back to high school, but the campus is so big that by the time I hobble to my next class, the class is over. The school system sends a tutor to home school me.

For me, there is no prom. There are no high-school dances, no football games, no hanging out with friends.

With little else to do, I work on my relationship with my mom. After years of fighting, I now rely on her 100 percent to take care of me. She changes my bedpans and washes my waist-length hair while I'm in my hospital bed. I can't run from her, so I stop being so hateful. We find a peace between us.

As I turn 17, the muscles in my leg are so atrophied that when I push the skin on my thigh, my finger goes right to the bone. But I still wake up every day in hopeful anticipation that this is the day something will change with my foot.

Watch me. I'll walk again.

ॐॐॐ

My mom and I sit in the waiting room, anxiously anticipating what the surgeon will tell us about my latest foot surgery, my ninth. This time, surgeons attach my foot to my leg to let skin grow from my leg to cover the bottom of my foot. I stare at the doctor, waiting for my verdict and silently defying him to tell me anything negative.

He reveals the news slowly.

"The surgery has worked, and you may be able to walk, but you won't be able to support yourself," he says. I'm not sure who is more disappointed — me or Mom. "You'll always be handicapped and need someone to help you on a daily basis."

We live in Texas now, as my parents have finally divorced, and my mom has taken me and my three siblings with her to live with my grandparents for good. As we get in the car to drive to their house, I can tell Mom is unhappy with the doctor's prognosis.

"There's no way you're living with me, Pam," she says, staring straight ahead, her hands keeping a tight grip on the steering wheel. She looks tired. "I am not taking care of you anymore."

Feelings I haven't felt in two years explode from their hiding places. The spirit of rebellion hasn't been quenched in my two bedridden years. It has just been asleep.

"Don't worry, Mom. You won't have to."

ॐॐॐ

The next morning, I call George, a 19-year-old boy I recently met at my grandparents' church. He is very interested in me, but until now, I haven't cared. I ask him to come over, and I plan to drop a bombshell on him.

"Do you remember saying you'd give anything to marry me? Let's do it."

The look on his sweet, naïve face is all the answer I need. I triumphantly tell my mom she doesn't have to take care of me anymore. When she asks me if I know what I'm doing, I answer, "Absolutely."

George doesn't waste any time. He buys an engagement ring that afternoon, a small diamond with two stones set on either side. Within weeks, I hobble on crutches down the aisle of my grandmother's church and become his wife.

Even I am not strong enough to keep up this façade; I start drinking so I can handle being with George. He is a kind Southern boy, but he's not the kind of guy who makes my stomach flutter or even piques my interest. When my aunt, who lives in Alaska, offers to fly us up there three months later — shortly after I have begun walking for the first time in two years — I jump at the chance to go to vocational school and start a new life.

Soon after George and I arrive, I start school, and I get a taste of what it can feel like to walk again without crutches, to learn new skills and get a job and support myself. I don't need George, whom I can hardly tolerate anymore. Weeks later, I sit down with my husband of four months and tell him we're finished. I don't have much to say.

"It's over, George. You need to go back to Texas. This marriage isn't true." I hand him a plane ticket my aunt bought him for a flight back to Texas the next day.

His face crumples into tears. He truly loves me, he says through his sobs. How can I do this to him? He stares at the paper ticket in disbelief.

This innocent boy just doesn't understand that I have simply misled him. All I want is my independence, and he needs to go. He's hurt too deeply to talk much more, and we hardly say goodbye the next day when he leaves with my aunt for the long drive to the airport.

శావావా

Several years later, I listen to my counselor telling me I am severely depressed, to the point where I'm nearly catatonic.

"I could put you in a hospital today. Is that what you want?"

"Of course not. I have a son, and I want to take care of him." I cross my arms and stare at the counselor. He leans forward.

"Yes? Well, you've got to fight like crazy."

After George flies back to Texas, I spend several years getting drunk and sleeping with men. I wouldn't call them relationships, more like encounters. I have long thought my body is meant to be used by men, so promiscuity feels right — as long as I drink a lot first. But I know in my heart this isn't what I really want, so I only choose men there's clearly no future with.

I marry two of these men, but neither lasts long. I have my son, Keegan, with my second husband, a drug addict and alcoholic I'm sure I can change with enough love. I only stay with my third husband a few months, quickly getting out of a relationship I could tell was on the way to becoming abusive.

At age 26, I am deeply ashamed of what I have done with men and marriage. It's hard to imagine I will ever be worthy of anything good in my life. I decide that I will become a single mom and that men will no longer be an answer for me. I may go out with a few, but I'm not getting serious with anyone.

I draw on that same strong will that helped me walk again to help me overcome depression. I refuse to take antidepressants because I want to be better without drugs.

ॐॐॐ

I hear a rustling noise, and I look up from my desk at the hotel to see the carpenter, who's been working on a remodeling job here, standing in front of me. We've talked a few times before. He's very nice, and he pours me coffee every day and makes small talk.

"I have tickets," he declares. "A promotional train is coming to take people to Anchorage and back for a day. I was wondering if you'd like to come with me."

Is this man asking me out on a date? I've never been on a "date" before. All I do is drink and have sex with men. Do I dare do something with such a nice, decent person who doesn't drink or take drugs?

"Can I think about that and call you?" I ask the

carpenter. He takes my odd request in stride and gives me his phone number. I find this idea of an actual date quite intriguing, but I need to decide if I'm ready for it. I finally have gotten my life together. I have a good job, and I'm supporting myself and Keegan. I've spent time with several men, but I'm not interested in them.

I call Robin the next day and accept. What could a day hurt?

We meet at 6 a.m. for the four-hour train ride to Anchorage. Robin takes me to a really nice restaurant, a first for me, and we go window shopping. There is nothing attached to it, and I have enjoyed our hours of conversation.

For our second date, Robin charters a sailboat. I hate sailing, and I'm not sure if I like Robin, but I'm curious about what goes on during these real dates. He asks me to meet him before dawn for our third date, breakfast and bird watching. This is the first man I've ever met who respects me and wants to spend time with me that doesn't involve drugs, drinking and sex. I've never known anything like it.

When I ask my mom, who has moved to Seward, to watch Keegan during that early-morning date, she bursts out laughing.

"Really, Pam, bird watching at 5 a.m.? Can you not come up with a better lie than that?" Mom is well aware of my history with men.

"Mom, that is what this man really asked me to do." I'm not sure if she believes me.

OUT OF THE SHADOWS

~~~~~

Six months later, I move into Robin's cabin in the woods. He's built this home himself, and I find his lifestyle on this beautiful and simple property seven miles outside Seward intriguing. The cabin is set off the road, surrounded by tall spruce trees. A babbling stream behind the house provides a soothing melody.

On Christmas morning, Robin presents me with a small wrapped box. Inside is a simple gold band. I'm a bit puzzled, but it's a nice ring, and I slip it on my right hand and hold it out for a better view.

"Thank you," I tell him, smiling at this token of friendship.

"You're welcome," he replies. The conversation moves on to other topics.

I am the assistant manager at a hotel, and my boss has worked all of the shifts today so employees can be with their families on Christmas. I feel sorry for my boss and appreciate his sacrifice on Christmas, so I ask Robin if I can take his Ford Bronco II into town to relieve my boss for an hour so he can at least eat Christmas dinner. The baby-blue vehicle handles the snow better than my car, and Robin readily agrees.

The Bronco is built for Alaska's rough weather, with two sets of gears. The second stick shift on the floor engages the four-wheel drive, which I definitely need to get through the thick layer of snow on the ground.

As I push the gear into position, a loud *crunch* echoes

through the vehicle, and it jerks to a stop. I sit in the driver's seat for a minute, trying to figure out what has happened and how I'm going to explain this to Robin.

Robin walks outside when he notices the Bronco is still parked by the cabin.

"Aren't you going to work?" he asks.

I take a deep breath. "Well, I tried to shift the gears, and something crunched, and now the car won't move." I brace myself for what I think I deserve, for Robin to yell at me and call me stupid for tearing up his car.

"What does that mean?" I ask quietly.

"Well, it means you're not going anywhere. And this truck is going to the shop tomorrow. The gears are stripped."

Relief washes over me as the seconds tick by, and Robin doesn't explode in anger.

This is the kind of man I can marry. He's not mad, just kind and patient.

When Robin brings the car back from the shop, he hands me a large metal gear, stripped bare of its teeth. I turn the gray disk over in my hand, wondering what it has to do with me or the car.

"Pam," Robin says, a grin playing on his face, "this is your diamond ring." I look at him quizzically. "I thought you gave the diamond ring on the day you marry since it's more expensive. And this car repair has cost me so much money that this will have to do for your diamond."

He breaks into a wide smile.

This kind, funny and understanding man had meant to

propose Christmas morning with that gold band, thinking it was the engagement ring. That afternoon, he had called my family, asking what he had done wrong when I didn't respond to the ring. They explained the mix-up.

Robin has himself escaped from a life of drinking, drugs and painful relationships. He cleaned up, treated himself to a trip to Hawaii, bought the Bronco and built his cabin in the woods. The last piece, he tells me, is finding someone to share his new life.

I say yes. I'm honored that he has chosen me.

We are married in the fall of 1987, and our daughter, Amy, is born the next year.

అందాల

One night after Robin and baby Amy have gone to bed, I sit quietly in our living room on the steps leading up to our bedroom. The cabin is so peaceful at night, the only sounds coming from the little stream outside. I bask in the contentedness of my new life.

Suddenly, I hear a voice in my head. I know who it is. I've known God since I was a child, but I've chosen not to follow him.

Won't you come back? I've been waiting for you.

I fall to my knees. My answer comes easily.

Okay, God. I'm coming. I won't turn back this time or run away.

I have been so afraid to go to church because I don't think I'm good enough, but God has given me a personal invitation here in my house. This is the safest, most beautiful place I know, where for the first time I am living a decent life free of drugs and alcohol. There are no preachers or pretenses, just me and God.

My issues with being good enough begin to unravel, as God shows me he loved me before I was even born. I begin to understand just how immense God's love is.

రోరోరో

Day by day, God begins repairing the physical, emotional and spiritual damage the world has done. My life takes a new turn.

God speaks again one day while I'm sitting at my computer, working at my high-paying job in inventory control at an accounting firm. The screen is filled with numbers I am reconciling.

How does this glorify me?

I stop typing and pause for a few moments to look at the computer, the endless numbers and the piles of paper on my desk.

Well, it doesn't, God.

Then give it up. Walk away.

Wait a minute. This job pays well, and what am I giving it up for?

God is sweetly gentle with me as I wrestle with his request. He gives us what we need to walk in this world, and I begin to think about children in foster care. When I ask Robin his opinion on me quitting my job, which brings in more than $3,000 a month, so that we can be foster parents, he's agreeable.

My employers are Christian people, and when I give them my six-month notice, they understand. God has a plan for me, I tell them, and I need to give up this job. God's plan is beautiful, and I easily walk away from money, career potential and a corporate life to see what will unfold.

Over the next 12 years, Robin and I foster 70 children in our home, which Robin adds on to as our family grows. In 1997, we adopt our son, Brian, who had suffered from fetal alcohol syndrome. I fill up my life with volunteering, parenting and serving on a local mental health board and as PTA president at my children's school.

❧❧❧

I peer in the mirror in my sister's bathroom and wonder what's wrong with my long brown hair. One side hits my chin, and the other side is down to my shoulder. I run my hands through both sides of my hair, which confirms that one side is noticeably thinner than the other. I would never let my hair get so lopsided and unkempt.

"Diana?" I call out. For some reason, I'm spending the day at her house. "What is wrong with my hair? It doesn't look right."

Diana stands in the bathroom door, a concerned look on her face. She takes a deep breath, and I can tell she has something important to tell me. "Um, Pam, you've had brain surgery." She steps back a little as I take in this news. "The doctors had to shave your head for the surgery, and the anti-seizure drugs you've taken have made some of your hair fall out."

This cannot be true. I am dumbfounded.

"I did not. Nobody would give me brain surgery. Are you crazy?"

"Let me show you," Diana says, stepping into the bathroom. Her face appears in the mirror next to mine.

"Lean your head forward." She gently parts my hair, revealing a long scar that travels from the top of my head to my ear.

"Who did this? Why would somebody do this to me?" My mind can hardly comprehend that my skull has been cut open, and someone has operated on my brain. How is this possible? And how is it possible that I don't know anything about it?

"Pam, you've had an aneurism."

Diana sounds like she's speaking another language, the medical terminology garbled in my ears. *Aneurism?* I've never heard that word before. *How do you spell it?* Reality does not fit with her words. I'm standing in my sister's house, perfectly fine except for my hair and this big scar, and she's telling me that I have been recovering from a brain aneurism. I don't remember experiencing any of this, but I can't argue with the scar. I sit down, as if the soft couch will help absorb some of the shock and confusion I'm feeling, and wait for Robin to pick me up.

OUT OF THE SHADOWS

කක

I run straight to the computer as soon as I set foot in our cabin and settle into the desk chair. Robin and the kids go to bed, but I hardly notice. I pull up Google and type in "aneurism." I read for hours, scrolling down the screen, and the printer hums as it spits out page after page about my medical condition.

I look at images of brain aneurisms, medical drawings, black-and-white brain scans and pictures taken during surgery with white arrows added to point out the potentially deadly blood clot. The computer screen glows late into the night as I click on pictures, examining each one and imagining such a thing in my own brain.

Several weeks pass as I try to understand what has happened. Everything around me is the same. Robin still goes to work. My children go to school. My clothes are hanging in my closet, the car is outside in the driveway. Normal life swirls around me as I learn about aneurisms and try to sort out what has led me here.

God speaks to me sweetly in the midst of my confusion and panic, his voice calming my frantic attempts to understand.

Don't be afraid. Whatever you hear, I was with you the whole time.

My last memory is of the day before I had the aneurism, so over the next few weeks, Robin and my family slowly fill in the last six months of my life.

THE CANARY SINGS

చచచ

One Sunday morning in May 2001, I am getting ready for work, and I go downstairs to wash my hair. Robin flies into the room when he hears me screaming to call 911. He finds me vomiting and convulsing on the floor, having seizures right in front of him.

We live in Seward, which is 120 long, arduous miles from Anchorage. There's no time for an ambulance, so Medivac flies me to a hospital in Anchorage, where doctors tell Robin they are surprised I am still alive. There is something very wrong with my brain, and my condition is too severe for this hospital to handle.

Robin flies with me on to Seattle, where medics on the plane aren't sure I will survive the ride.

Doctors tell my family I am not going to live, so my sister, mother, father and brothers fly to Seattle to be with me. I've seen pictures of myself from these days, barely recognizable under the wires and tubes snaking from my body, hooking me to ventilators and respirators and other life-preserving machines.

These days are so hard on my family, who have rented an apartment near the hospital and settled in for the long term. They sit in anguish in the waiting room day after day, surgery after surgery, where doctors say the procedure can kill me. Thirty percent of the people who have my type of aneurism live, and most of those who do never again function on their own.

A month after my aneurism, I'm amazingly ready for

rehab. My family convinces doctors to let me go back to Anchorage, where I am taught to walk, talk and function again. When I come home, someone has to be with me at all times in case I do something crazy, like forget to turn the stove off and set the house on fire.

Diana knew that things weren't right with me during those six months. Once, I glare at her and ask who that woman is with my sister's husband. I somehow recognize Diana's husband, but at the moment I have no idea who the woman, my sister, in front of me is. Another time, after watching an episode of *I Love Lucy*, where Lucy is pregnant, I tell everyone I am in the hospital because the baby died.

It's a powerful thing, what can happen to your mind.

ক্তক্তক্ত

A year after my aneurism, Mom and I are sitting in the office of Dr. David Newell, the surgeon who was in charge of my case in Seattle. I have read every detail of my medical records from Harbor View Hospital trying to reconstruct what happened to me, but I still worry that I'm not really healed, or worse, it might happen again. Mom and I have toured the hospital, I've seen my room in the Intensive Care Unit with all of the tubes and wires to sustain life and met the nurses who cared for me. I don't remember any of it.

I don't remember this surgeon, either, a kindly man with glasses and a receding hairline. He gives me a long stare as he comes into the room, like he's looking at someone from another world.

"Do you realize that 70 percent of people with your type of aneurism die immediately? And that those who do live do not function — and that you should not be standing here?"

"Yeah." I do understand, but it's still hard to comprehend the miracle that's happened.

Then Dr. Newell surprises me. His professional look falls away, and his face softens.

"Can I have a hug?"

Of course he can. We embrace, someone who should have died and the surgeon who helped save her life.

Dr. Newell pulls a camera out of his desk, and I stand, grinning as he takes my picture. He wants to share it with his colleagues, show them the patient who defied odds and death.

"This doesn't happen, Pam. I remember I had no hope for you."

I look at him. "Do you believe in God?" The fact that I could live through a brain aneurism is not without divine intervention.

Dr. Newell just smiles, and then he gives me another hug.

❧❧❧

In the three years before my aneurism, I had a secret. On the outside, I was a regular churchgoer, a community leader, a dedicated mom. But I had begun to put God on the backburner, and I was spiritually hanging by a thread. I still went to church faithfully at Eagle's Nest Christian Fellowship, just sitting there, pretending to listen. I didn't want anybody to know that God and I were hardly talking.

If I had died that day in May, I'm honestly not sure where my soul would have gone.

Diana kept a journal during my aneurism and recovery, even writing down her prayers. I learned that all of the churches in Seward called out to God on my behalf. I was in no position to pray for myself, but every denomination in my little town was praying for me.

For some reason, God had chosen to spare me. Death was hanging right there, and God said, *No, no, she gets more time.*

Spiritually, I was awakened in a way I never knew was possible. As I tried to recreate the six months that I lost, God assured me that he had been with me the whole time and that he had something in store for me. It was so new and so fresh. My body had been healed, and so had my mind and spirit. It was so beautiful and so personal, and I felt as if I could breathe and walk again. It was time for the canary to sing.

God, I am going to live as I have never lived before. I am going to take joy in every single breath that is given to me for the rest of my life. When it is my time, it will truly be my appointed time.

THE CANARY SINGS

కాలుజాలు

Life since my aneurism has not been without trials and tribulations, but God has given me a new way of dealing with the hardest times. Much of life has been beautiful, as I now have three grandchildren and am a children's ministry leader at my church, Eagle's Nest Christian Fellowship.

God gave me Romans 8:28 after the aneurism. I held on to this verse through trials afterward: "And we know that in all things God works for the good of those who love him, who have been called according to his purpose."

Sometimes people notice that I walk with a slight limp, and many days my foot hurts and limits what I can do physically. I learned long ago to walk on the ball of my foot since a lot of my heel is missing, but my modified walk will never let me forget that day in the field behind my house.

I would not give up my severed heel for anything. I take great pleasure in it because I know that I probably would not be alive, that I would have died during my rebellion, if it wasn't for God's intervention. It reminds me of God's extreme mercy over me.

Once I could think through complicated accounting problems and do several tasks at once. My aneurism has limited my brain's capacity, and now I can only focus on one thing at a time. But I would welcome a dozen aneurisms if the reward was the amazing faith in God and renewed spirit that I received after the one aneurism I had.

OUT OF THE SHADOWS

I have a new purpose ministering to children, and every breath I take is precious. God has equipped me to truly overcome anything and everything that this world can offer, and he has opened up a world I never dreamed of. My whole life goal is to love him with all my heart, soul and spirit. He wouldn't have brought me back for nothing.

ABANDONED NO MORE
The Story of Dana Goodwater
Written by Jason Chatraw

Boys' Town. It sounds like it could be a fun place, but I knew differently. Just evoking those two words consecutively was enough to create a sudden rush of fear. Boys' Town was a home for boys who needed the iron fist of discipline to help them behave. And my dad was threatening to send me there.

The anxious moments that followed my dad's threat were unnerving. He packed me a suitcase, placed it by the door and issued a stern warning.

"Son, if you ever act up again, I'm going to drop you off at Boys' Town."

I was 5 years old.

છે છે છે

This event became etched into my mind, and it traumatized me. Confused in my fragile state, I couldn't tell if my father was merely threatening me or if he was serious. I don't even remember what I did. Most of my mischievous acts occurred while I was under the watchful eye of my mom at home.

However, when my dad spoke, I took him seriously — and I certainly didn't want to discover that he was joking, even if he was.

OUT OF THE SHADOWS

Not knowing whether the person who brought you into the world is going to continue to receive you or take you some place to let other people "deal with you" — that would be unnerving for any child of any age. I feared being abandoned and unaccepted. I can verbalize how I felt now, but I couldn't then. I was terrified.

In an instant, a new worldview formed in my mind: *Make a misstep and you will be abandoned.*

Performance soon became my elixir for such nightmares. It was the only way to stave off such terrifying fears. And a dangerous die was cast for my life.

≈≈≈

Having risen through the ranks of a finance company to become vice-president, my dad was in charge of five different branches in a couple of different regions. That meant my mom became the primary caretaker for me, my brother and my two sisters. We kids stuck together and grew really close over the years. And while my mom managed the best she could, my dad's absence in the home was glaring.

The only times we saw my dad were on the weekends when he came home from his weeklong business trips throughout the regions he oversaw. Unfortunately, his time home usually consisted of being the enforcer after my mom detailed all our disobedient acts over the previous week. I was desperate for the attention of someone, anyone — the kind of attention that isn't found on the business end of a belt. So I began looking toward my brother.

My brother was five years older than me, and he viewed me as a pest instead of a potential ally. He was trying to be cool with his friends, so why would he want his kid brother around? He did his best to drive me away, calling me names like "stupid" and "idiot." That might sound like normal sibling banter to most, but I knew that there was something else to the name-calling; I just wasn't sure what it was. His attempt to push me away was somewhat successful. After all, if you know your big brother doesn't want to be around you, why would you want to be around him and suffer the verbal abuse?

I continued searching for someone to confide in, a place that was safe to go. I tried with my sisters, but personality and age difference nixed the idea. Meanwhile the notion continued to grow in my head: I was an idiot. I became an introvert. I didn't want to be like this, but constructing a walled fortress seemed like the best way to protect myself from further rejection. It was also a way I could lessen the damaging voices that proclaimed me to be stupid.

Reflecting now about these formative years in my thinking, I don't blame my parents or my siblings. The paradigm of fearing a swift kick to the curb, of feeling that I was stupid — those were things that were introduced into my life by others but became ideas that I cultivated into "factual" statements about who I was over time. They became a powerful force in my life.

OUT OF THE SHADOWS

❧❧❧

As I headed into my sixth-grade year, my feelings of abandonment were nearing the point of no return when my parents announced they were separating.

This was a dark year in my life, the time when life became completely unstable and disjointed for me. My parents had been fighting and threatening to divorce each other for quite some time. And, of course, we kids heard everything. Whether we were around or not made no difference to my parents. They spoke their mind about the other spouse freely. Listening to these tête-a-têtes that should not have been for our ears began to cause us all to question our role in why our parents weren't getting along. We all wondered to ourselves if it was our fault, rarely speaking of our home that was quickly crumbling.

It was hard on all of us, but its impact on me was substantial and evident. My grades plunged. I took this freefall hard and couldn't shake it.

When my mom finally moved out, we didn't get a choice about where we would live. In order to keep some sense of normalcy, we stayed with my dad at home.

I remember feeling this intense hurt and anger in my heart that my mom and dad weren't together, as I desperately wanted them to stay together. We all felt an impact on some level — and we all dealt with it differently.

During my sixth-grade year, I found I could gain the acceptance I craved from some older boys on our block.

They were about four or five years older than me and quickly befriended me. I was more than a passing interest to this group of guys — and they certainly didn't treat me the way my brother did. To them, I wasn't a bratty kid brother. Instead, I was their protégé, someone they chose to take under their tutelage and educate in the ways of the world. One of those educational moments included alcohol.

During a party my parents hosted, I found a spot hidden beneath the pool table and drank my first beer. All the talk about alcohol by my older friends emboldened me. We began the practice of stealing liquor out of one of my friend's neighbors' garage. Stashing the bottle, we would guzzle it before going out to attend teen dances. We would be really drunk and act stupid. It was the only way to get me out of the tough introverted shell I had constructed. If I looked stupid, I was fine with it because I had an excuse now — it was the alcohol that made me do it. I became free to act however I wanted.

After sixth grade, my parents finally reconciled, and my mom returned home. Unfortunately, the damage was already done. While I was pleased that they decided to reunite, I had already determined not to waste my time trying to earn their approval when I already had it with my older friends, no matter how poor an influence they were on me.

ॐॐॐ

I found a healthy dose of the acceptance I was looking for on athletic playing fields. My identity began to center around my ability to excel as an athlete. I started wrestling and playing football, quickly discovering that I was pretty good at both sports. After excelling in both in junior high, I dumped wrestling for football after I discovered which sport garnered more glory from my peers. Then I determined to play on the collegiate level.

As my success on the field rose, so did the acceptance of others. After games, when we would go out and party, people recognized me and would heap praise on me. It was fun to wallow in the adulation of my peers. While I knew that I was accepted, I still never felt that I was free to be myself until I had consumed a sufficient amount of alcohol.

In high school, most of my relationships developed as a direct result of my involvement in sports. It brought me friends and girlfriends. Sports brought me attention, acceptance and approval. Meanwhile, it also validated the paradigm that had developed in my mind: *Perform well and you will be loved.*

My athletic skills were good enough to warrant interest from a handful of colleges. Collegiate coaches began poking around and asking about my background and, more importantly, my grades.

When I was in high school, I didn't apply myself. After all, I was stupid, right? It was enough to derail my dream of playing college football. As badly as I wanted to continue this attention from others due to my athletic ability, playing collegiately carried with it the obligation of having sufficient grades and a suitable test score. While they weren't honor-roll material, my grades were enough to qualify me to play in college. My ACT score became the remaining piece of information that I refused to satisfy.

Interested college coaches would ask me to fill out a questionnaire and eventually follow up with one glaring question: Why didn't you fill out the blank where your ACT score goes? But I had yet to take this test.

Honestly, I didn't want to know if I was really that stupid. The seeds of the lies spoken over me at a young age had now blossomed into full-grown rejection on my part, though I was reluctant to confirm it. I thought if I just didn't know, then maybe it wasn't true, even though deep down I thought it was.

Long after my window of opportunity to play college sports vanished, I took the ACT and proved myself wrong, scoring high enough to earn admission to a university. But I didn't last long due to the grip alcohol had on my life.

ॐॐॐ

As I excelled on the playing field, I struggled in other areas of my life. My growing addiction to alcohol led me to some dark places my senior year, including the way I got into a drunken fight.

One night I was drunk at a high school graduation party with some friends when someone hit me in the face with his fist. I turned around to see a guy take off running

— so I pursued him. He jumped in his car and started driving home, and I followed him with my friends. When we got to his house, we started to fight. Furious at what he had done to me, I hit him hard in the side of the face, and he started convulsing. I thought, *Oh, man. I killed this guy!* Then before we could figure out what was going on, his dad, who was a local police officer, stormed outside with a gun and started firing into the air.

As I stood there, his dad came and pointed the gun at my head and kneed me in the groin. I was scared for my life.

Eventually, the officer let me up, but I was already experiencing overwhelming feelings of regret. I got my friends to take me home. The influence alcohol had over my life was starting to result in some devastating consequences, none more so than when I lost one of my friends to suicide.

One of my good friends who used to drink with our group got really drunk one night and shot himself in the head. While already struggling with feelings of guilt that I somehow contributed to his demise, I couldn't shake the fact that my friend chose one of our favorite drinking spots in the woods as the location for his suicide. His death shattered my world.

Getting a call from his little brother to deliver the news was probably one of the hardest things I ever had to hear. Adding to my guilt was the fact that my friend had even called me in recent weeks preceding his death, asking me questions about what would happen to him if he committed suicide. With my limited Catholic background, I warned him that any such action would result in an eternity in hell and advised him not to do it. No one took him seriously, especially me. But that didn't stop me from rehashing every conversation in my head and wondering what I could have said differently to persuade him not to take his life.

It was a big wake-up call for me. I began pondering about the hereafter as I wondered where my friend was. It was at that moment when I began to do some soul searching. I can't say that God just *totally* broke in. I still hadn't chosen to give my life to Christ, as I was still doing my own thing. But it definitely touched me to the extent that I asked questions about where I might go. Was I going to go to hell? Or purgatory, as I was taught as a Catholic? I didn't know what to believe. The only thing I really knew about God or the Bible were the Ten Commandments and Jesus at Easter. At that pivotal moment, I began searching.

かかか

While we had oscillated between Colorado and Nebraska growing up due to my dad's job, I remained in Nebraska following high school for a few years before heading back to Colorado to work. I began working as a roofer and trying to sort out my life.

It didn't take too long before God finally arrested me in the only way that I could have been arrested — to experience his love in the most unconditional of ways.

One day I received word that my best friend Matt's sister, Jenny, had been diagnosed with cancer. She was 14 years old — and a devout Christian. I returned to Nebraska to visit her. She was such a beautiful little girl, but the effects of cancer were ravaging her body. I barely recognized her face the final time I saw her, but her heart remained the same.

Jenny's mom and dad told me that Jenny had quit praying for herself and started praying for five people that she knew who needed a relationship with God. Her act of love floored me. Why? Why quit praying for yourself and pray for one of your brother's friends? Why waste your time praying for others? It was a great act of love, and it left a lasting impression on me. Throughout my life, a few people had been bold enough to share the good news of God's love for me, but those were just words, seeds being planted in my heart to be harvested at the right time. The right time was Jenny's funeral.

At the funeral, a pastor preached the salvation message. After he finished speaking, he asked if anybody wanted to begin a relationship with Jesus. At that moment, something stirred in me. I knew I had to make the decision to do this. My heart was overwhelmed by the realization of God's love for me, a love that wasn't based on how well I behaved but purely on the fact that I was his creation. I understood it was a love that couldn't be earned or won. It was freely given.

I don't even remember what the prayer was, but I do

recall confessing Jesus as my Lord and Savior with my mouth and believing in my heart. My life was about to be turned upside down. I had been adopted into God's family.

❧❧❧

Almost immediately, I felt that I needed to stop hanging out with my friends who weren't influencing me in a positive way. I stopped drinking and smoking pot. It was easy to shed those worldly things. Even the promiscuous lifestyle I had been leading was washed away in the midst of God's overwhelming love. I truly felt born again.

This decision started a major shift for me in my thinking. When I thought about the Bible, the stories in the Old Testament were what readily came to mind. I saw a God who was pretty rough and dealt severely with sin. His judgment was harsh. But now, my perspective didn't seem correct.

I began seeing God in a new light, one who encouraged us to abide by his word. But it wasn't easy for me. I thought it was impossible to live by the Ten Commandments, although I was trying very hard. I wanted to live that way, but knew I was setting myself up for failure. Based on my old paradigm, I knew it was only a matter of time before I slipped up and did something that angered God and caused him to disown me.

The more I sinned, the more I wanted to stop doing it.

There was a tug of war with the flesh. I just kept waiting for God to say, "Enough. No more! We're severing our relationship." That was a real fear in my life, but a very unhealthy fear. It spilled over into my life and developed into what I call "ruts in my brain." I was still trying to secure trust and acceptance. Even though I had accepted Christ, I wondered what fully trusting him would look like. I believed that if I lied or looked at a woman lustfully, I was going to be disowned by God.

I knew that salvation was a free gift. But I believed that I had to work hard to keep it. As I struggled to let go of different habits in my life that were destructive, I had a hard time believing I could share my faith in a meaningful way. I would pray, "God, if you don't break into this thought pattern and show me how to stop, there is no way I can sit here and testify about your goodness, your power and your love — especially if I don't understand it completely."

I still felt there was something I was supposed to do. But I didn't know what to do. Many times, I asked God to take something out of my life and help me conquer it. I wanted God to either help me conquer those destructive behaviors in my life or take me from this earth. I didn't fully understand what God's love covered and what it did for me now. That was the treadmill I was running on in my life, and I was getting nowhere.

"The prayer of a righteous man is powerful and effective" (James 5:16).

I believe the Lord said to me, "I hear your heart, and I'm going to begin to show you some things." He told me to simply be as a child. That disarmed me a little bit; my whole mentality was *Do, do, do.* I thought I had to do this and do that — *I've got to pray and I've got to read the Bible and I've got to worship and I've got to show up at church.* I was so busy *doing* that I never had a chance to simply *be* as a child. I needed him to disarm me. I wanted to earn his acceptance and approval — but that was impossible. I had nothing to prove to him. So, he came after me. When I messed up, he didn't kick me to the curb. He gently loved me. And then I experienced God's unconditional love in the form of another person.

❧❧❧

As I was still grappling with these issues in my faith, I continued to deepen my relationship with God. I knew I wanted to follow him, even though it wasn't always easy. Then one morning at a church missions convention, a missionary from Mexico preached on the will of God. As he was preaching, I felt as though God physically lassoed my stomach and pulled me down to the altar. On that day, this little man from Mexico knelt down next to me and began to tell me that the Lord was calling me to share the Gospel. His word confirmed what I had already been sensing: God was calling me to the ministry.

I met with my pastor to discuss the new calling in my life, and he had a shocking piece of advice for me.

"If you're called to the ministry, Dana, you need to get married, for plenty of good reasons."

I sat quietly pondering his statement before he dispensed with the small talk.

"So, who are you interested in?"

I was 26 at the time and actively involved in our singles ministry. I was happy and content there, but there was this woman named Debbie who served on the singles leadership team and interested me. But I was reluctant to tell my pastor.

With a little prodding, I finally relented and told him that I was having feelings for a woman on our singles ministry team but didn't reveal her name.

"We're praying together during these meetings, and, before you know it, my mind is drifting," I told him. "To be honest with you, my feelings for her are starting to hinder me from worshiping the Lord."

"Well, who is it?" he fired back, with his curiosity fully piqued.

I finally let her name slip — and he began laughing.

"You know what? She came up to me and told me the exact same thing about you," he said, reveling in the moment.

Debbie and I had no idea that we both felt that way about each other.

Not one for long and drawn-out engagements, my pastor continued, "I think you should tell her at the next singles meeting."

So I did.

I sat down with Debbie and began to pour out my heart. I told her that I'd been through the whole dating scene and wasn't interested in it anymore. I told her that I knew in my heart she was the one.

"Let's just skip right over the dating part and get married," I told her.

Five months later, we were married. And it was through her that I began to see God's love and grace and forgiveness in a whole new light.

❧❧❧

When I told my wife that I looked at pornography, it was the first time that I ever saw God's love with skin on it. I had never seen it displayed toward me from another human being. And God used that moment to teach me a lot.

As I was growing up, my dad never left me or forsook me, but I always had that fear. Today, we have a great relationship, but that's only happened as a result of a lot of healing that has taken place in our relationship because God has changed my heart.

I learned a lot about forgiveness through the process of reconciliation. I stopped trying to earn other people's approval and became more childlike in my faith. And then I watched Debbie model God's forgiveness and his heart toward me.

After I confessed to her about my struggles, I looked into her eyes and saw the love of God. She didn't *react* —

she *responded.* I was fully prepared for her to kick me to the curb. *There goes my marriage.*

"Dana, I love you more now than I ever have," she finally said.

I couldn't understand that. She said she felt closer to me now than she ever had. God began to use that in my life in a powerful way — love with skin on it. I already knew there was a God, but he came alive to me in a new and exciting way as I watched him flow through my wife. I began to see what God's heart was like.

అఅఅ

Despite the way I struggled with doubt and wanted to experience full freedom in my relationship with God, he never stopped coming after me. As I studied the Old Testament, I saw God as harsh in his judgment toward people. But God began to unravel that Old Testament paradigm in my mind.

As I was praying and meditating about this change taking place in my life, God revealed some life-changing concepts to me, shaking up my old worldview. Jesus went around helping the sick and helping the poor — that was different than a harsh, judgmental God. He began to flood me with many different thoughts of love. And I began to respond.

I saw God's love with my own eyes through my wife. I knew I had to escape these ruts in my brain and find a new track. God was knocking me off course and into this new way of thinking. He began to show me who he was and his great love toward me.

While it can be wrapped up in a few neat paragraphs, this transformation didn't happen overnight. It was a series of events and long stretches of praying about these various ideas. Week after week, God affirmed his word to me and enabled me to understand more fully who he was. In the midst of my messing up and blowing it time and time again, he began to show me some of his other servants who blew it — men and women whom he forgave and didn't abandon. My past failures didn't have to influence my future anymore.

For so long, I had tried to change myself. But over time, I became free of that unattainable goal. I couldn't change myself — but God could change me. And he did.

I began to understand what it meant to be God's adopted son. It was an understanding that started another surprising event in my life.

৵৵৵৵

After five years of marriage, Debbie and I did not have any children. But that wasn't for lack of trying. I wanted to be able to express God's love toward my own children, maybe even grasping a new element of God's character in the process. So I approached Debbie about the idea of adoption. Much to my disappointment, she emphatically refused to entertain the idea.

She asked me a shocking question.

"How could I love another child as much as my own?"

I couldn't fathom those words coming out of her mouth. After all, I had been the beneficiary of God's amazing love flowing through her life so many times. And I wasn't her child! I challenged her thought process, but she resisted. Instead of pushing her on it, I stopped talking with her about it.

Just about the same time we were having these conversations, a missions team headed for Haiti for a short-term trip invited us to join them. They asked me to speak at a few meetings while we were there, and I agreed.

One afternoon, our team was scheduled to attend an orphanage there and help out with some of the kids. I opted to stay behind and prepare for my sermon later that evening.

Later that afternoon before the meeting, my wife came back visibly shaken. She was teary-eyed and struggled to explain the emotions that were obviously overwhelming her.

"Dana, I don't know what God is doing, but I know he loves this young girl from Haiti whom I met — and I am so broken over it."

I couldn't believe my ears, but I continued listening.

"Maybe God is asking me to do more than just support her. I think he might want us to adopt her."

I was excited but told her if that was the case, I wanted to meet this girl. So the day before we left, we traveled to the orphanage to meet her. It was an incredible time — there was just this connection.

As we boarded the plane for our flight home, we felt as if we were leaving our daughter behind in Haiti. While we felt strongly that this was the Lord, we wanted to make sure it wasn't just an emotional moment. So we continued asking the Lord for confirmation.

Not long after we returned, a friend of ours said, "We can't make this Steven Curtis Chapman concert tonight. Our boys want to go really badly, though. Would you mind taking them for us?"

We agreed and were floored when Steven Curtis Chapman paused from the normal flow of his concert to talk about his two adopted children and encourage others to investigate adoption if God was calling them to do it.

"If you ever felt like adopting and didn't feel you had enough love in your heart to love another child, there's something supernatural about it, and there's nothing like it," Chapman explained from the stage.

Debbie and I looked at each other in disbelief.

Shortly after, we started the adoption process. For nearly two years, we wrangled with adoption officials over proper documentation and waded through a situation with a corrupt orphanage director.

Frustrated, we decided to go to Haiti to help resolve the situation more quickly. Before leaving, we were warned that it would take another year before we could get our daughter home.

In just 17 days, we managed to secure all the proper documents, and a week later, Debbie brought our daughter home.

In the meantime, Debbie was fighting through a nasty virus — or so she thought.

Though Debbie was suffering from flu-like symptoms, her doctor only prescribed some medication, because Debbie flatly denied the possibility she could be pregnant. Two weeks after Debbie flew to Haiti to finalize the adoption and bring our daughter home, she learned she was pregnant.

Now, our hearts are full of love — equal love for both our children, and now, for all four of our children!

God has changed my life forever by his unconditional love. Every day I live in his light that brings ever-increasing transformation and a desire to see others find their true life from him.

PANIGA, MY DAUGHTER
The Story of Gert
Written by Arlene Showalter

There it is again.

While I folded laundry, a vision of a single dime rose and floated, in slow motion, before my eyes. Quicker than the harpoon thrust of my dad on a seal hunt, the truth pierced my heart.

Hush money.

❧ ❧ ❧

I am Inupiaq. My mother and father taught me the ways of our people as they had been taught by their own parents and their parents before them — traditions that stretch beyond recorded history. Those ways bound us as firmly together as ice binds continents during an arctic winter.

"Come, Paniga." Dad loved to call me *Daughter* in his native tongue. "It's time to check our nets."

I slipped out of bed and into the warm trousers Mom had made me from caribou hide from Dad's last hunt. Then I stepped into my mukluks, also made by Mom, digging my toes deep into the warm depths.

Mom worked on the other side of the room, preparing sourdough pancakes and fried trout for breakfast. I lifted my nose and inhaled.

"Smells wonderful."

"Yes," my dad agreed.

"Eat while it's hot." Mom gestured toward the table. "You've a long day ahead of you."

Dad and I shrugged into our warm parkas and stepped into the chill air, hurrying toward his nets. No sunshine would greet us today ... or tomorrow ... or the next day. Many weeks must pass before the sun's rays touched and warmed our faces again.

I hoped Dad's nets captured many ptarmigans today. This small grouse has brown feathers in the summer to hide in the tundra grass, but in winter its feathers turn snowy white. As with other foods harvested from the land and sea, the ptarmigan often saved our people from total starvation.

We worked in silence, freeing Dad's catch from the nets. I watched his strong, sure hands and studied his kind, broad face.

Dad — my teacher, protector and friend. I recalled when I was about 5 years old a discussion between him and Mom as she filled out the application for my social security number.

"What name should we put down?" she asked. "Gertrude Auliye or Gertrude Sookiayak?"

I'm Gert Auliye, just like Mom and Dad!

My parents never told me they were my grandparents or that their daughter, Erma, had written them a letter, asking them to keep me when I was born. Her husband was in the military service, stationed in Guam at the time.

PANIGA, MY DAUGHTER

I remembered that when I was about 5 years old, I saw my adoptive mother crying and crying. Years later, I wondered if that was when my birth mother had died, while giving birth to her 11th child.

Neither Mom nor Dad ever spoke of it. Nor did they ever explain the circumstances of my adoption.

"It's time to meet your real dad," my parents said to me a little while later. "His name is Henry, and he is here in Koyuk, visiting a friend, Kenneth Dewey." They pointed to a house. "Over there."

A real dad? I rushed to the house, knocked on the door and entered. Kids and noise swirled about me, but I could only stare at the man sitting in the middle of the chaos, like an island in a sea of tempest.

He smiled. I stared more. *This is my real dad?*

The tall thin man kept smiling.

Finally, I smiled back.

Nobody mentioned a real mother. Even in the excitement of meeting another father, my 5-year-old mind spun.

The Inupiaq life is hard. One does not speak of sad times or bad times. Energy is saved to hunt and fish and gather berries and greens to survive the long, harsh winters.

"Daughter, your hands grow idle." Dad's soft laugh jerked me back to the job at hand. We packed up the last of the ptarmigans and turned toward home. Mom would pluck and prepare the birds for storage.

My father excelled at hunting. Beluga whales, seals,

fish, moose, caribou. Their meat sustained us. Their hides clothed us.

Mom taught me how to weave herring in a circle of grass and hang it to dry. Dad and I used a two-man saw to harvest wood for our winter fires. We were a team — a tight trio of love.

When I was about 10, my parents' son returned from the Navy. How handsome he looked in his white hat and uniform. Our small home buzzed with excitement.

Soon after his homecoming, a storm blew in from the south. The south winds eroded certain banks, sometimes exposing mastodon fossils.

A few days later, we packed our boat and headed to our special camping spot behind Cape Dexter. After helping our parents set up camp, my brother and I hurried to the bank in search of fossils. Soon we had wandered far from our folks.

"Hey," my brother said, wrapping me in a hug. "I've missed you." With that, he slid a hand down, down, down into my trousers.

Shock, anger and fear pulsed through my veins. I fought. I screamed.

He struggled to hold me, grasping and groping.

I screamed harder, twisting and fighting until I had broken loose. My feet flew over the ground like a hunted snowshoe rabbit.

When my brother returned to camp, I could not look at him without disgust. I avoided him forever after that.

My parents seemed not to notice my strained behavior.

PANIGA, MY DAUGHTER

They asked no questions. I searched their kind yet inscrutable faces. Silence smothered me.

ೲೲೲ

Seven years later, I sat on our front porch, smoking. Across the street a young man sat, also smoking. He waved. I waved.

The village of Shaktoolik lies on a narrow strip of land with only two rows of houses. A river flowed behind our home. The ocean pounded behind his house.

The nightly ritual of smoking and waving turned into chats on each other's porches. That turned into dating. Then I got pregnant.

"You can't live together," Isaiah's father informed him. "You must marry."

So, when he came home, he said to me, "Let's get married on September 18."

I shrugged. "Okay."

We married. Our son, Jacob, was born two months later.

We flew to Nome for Jacob's birth. The moment he arrived, the room erupted with activity. Doctors and nurses surrounded me, repairing major tears. Others flocked around my tiny son.

"He's not breathing!" a doctor shouted. The nurse reached for the nearest oxygen tank.

Empty.

The team rushed my baby to the nurses' station, with

Isaiah hard on their heels. The nurse grabbed the tank there.

Empty. They ran from room to room, seeking a filled tank.

The next morning, Dr. Londborg came into my room during her rounds. "Call your husband," she ordered me. "I need to talk to you both."

Isaiah arrived less than 30 minutes later.

"We've done all we can for your baby," Dr. Londborg said. "He's not going to make it."

I looked at Isaiah. "I'll call Pastor Peterson," he said. Soon every church in the Norton Sound area was praying for our baby.

"If he survives the night," Dr. Londborg said, "we'll fly him to Anchorage for more specialized care."

The people continued praying.

The next morning, Dr. Londborg returned to my room, shaking her head. "We don't know what happened," she began, "but your son is doing better. So much so, we've decided to keep him here in Nome."

We returned to Shaktoolik with our miracle baby. A newborn cousin joined our family two months later. As the months passed, I realized something was wrong with my own son. The cousin quickly learned to roll over and then sit up. Jacob could do neither. The oxygen deprivation at birth had caused permanent brain damage.

Still, life was good.

Isaiah and I worked side by side, hunting, fishing and gathering. We picked berries, collected greens and wild rhubarb. We stayed active in our parents' church as well.

Jacob became ill two years later. After a few days, his conditioned worsened. We had to Medivac him to Nome where he was hospitalized for five days.

"This isn't going to work," I said to Isaiah after we returned to Shaktoolik. "We can't afford to charter a plane to Nome every time Jacob gets sick."

"You're right," he agreed. "Perhaps we should move there, to be close to the hospital."

After our move, we found a church home, attending the Nome Covenant Church. We stayed involved until alcohol overran our lives.

Soon we began social drinking with friends, which turned into shooting pool and bar-hopping. The further I drifted from God, the more miserable I became. Drink deadened the sadness and depression.

ȣȣȣ

We moved from Nome to Seward in 1988. Soon after, I experienced the vision of the floating dime for the first time, but brushed it from my mind. For three years, this same vision returned from time to time. Life and tending to four children crowded its meaning from me.

As I continued pulling wet laundry from my washer, the dime rose and floated about, hovering in front of my eyes with lazy grace. But this time, the vision continued. I saw a large brown hand place that dime in my hand — my baby hand. I stared at it.

OUT OF THE SHADOWS

My heart pounded. Suddenly, I knew whose hand had pressed that dime into my own. A male relative. Other hands appeared — family's hands, neighbors' hands, grown and almost grown, all groping, stroking, invading.

Familiar faces paired with the hands. I stared at my daughter's garment, strangled in my grip. Understanding dawned. Nobody would touch her as I had been touched.

Ever.

࿐࿐࿐

"Would you like to go to church with me?" Tami asked one day. She had been attending her best friend Dana's church. I hesitated and then agreed. I desperately needed a refuge. I had once experienced the baptism of the Holy Spirit, back in high school. I wanted to find him again.

My dad had died. I had four children and a struggling marriage. And I needed to keep tight rein on those memories.

Soon my children and I were regulars at the Assembly of God every Sunday and Wednesday. I worked hard at being a godly wife and mother, but sadness pressed me down. Many times I hid out in my bedroom, alone with God and my Bible, searching for him and his peace.

My biological father, Henry, died in July of 1997. He and I had kept in touch over the years, so I felt the loss keenly.

Two months later, I heard the phone ring while soaking in the tub. My son answered.

"She's not available right now," he said.

I toweled off, dressed and went to find my son.

"Who called?" I asked.

"Cheryl," he replied.

I dialed my friend's number.

"Hi, Cheryl," I said. "What did you need?"

"What?" Cheryl asked.

"You just called," I said.

"No, I didn't," she replied.

The only other Cheryl I knew worked in the nursing home where Mom lived.

I dialed the number.

"Hi, Cheryl," I said when she came to the phone. "Did you call me a few minutes ago?"

"Yes," she replied. "Your mother was transported to Anchorage for heart failure."

"When?" I gasped.

"Twelve hours ago."

I loaded my children into my Suburban, furious that nobody had bothered to inform me before now. I turned my car toward the highway, sighing at the two-and-a-half-hour drive ahead of us.

"Gert, I'm going to take your mother."

The car clock registered 9:21 p.m.

Lord, if you're going to take her, could you at least wait until I can say goodbye?

We arrived at the hospital and rushed to her room. Mom lay in a fetal position, sucking her thumb.

"I'm here, Mom." I leaned over the bedrail to hug her.

She said nothing, but a tear worked its way from her eye and slid down one cheek.

She knows it's me. It's enough.

I sat next to her, singing the choruses she loved and reading special verses from the Bible.

I struggled with fury over the doctors for not contacting me, fear of losing my mother and hope that she would pull through. I started looking into moving her to a nursing home in Seward.

I returned to the motel late. I awakened late but resting in God's peace. Somehow I knew he would give me more time with her.

But when I returned to the hospital, I knew something was terribly wrong. My mom lay gasping for breath. She looked at me and then closed her eyes in death. I lay next to her while her life ebbed away.

All my hope died with her.

Mother was the last person who truly loved me, I thought while I scrutinized the drink before me, slowly swirling its contents.

I'm tired of fighting for a dying marriage. I'm tired of trying to be the perfect wife and mother. I'm tired.

I celebrated my 37th birthday by turning from God and downing that drink. And another. And another.

The next 12 months passed in a thick fog of unfathomable depression.

I can't live like this anymore, my aching heart cried out … to nobody. I awoke on my 38th birthday thinking, *I've got to get help or get out.*

PANIGA, MY DAUGHTER

I moved to Nome, and after I got a good job and settled in a three-bedroom apartment, I returned to Seward for the three youngest children.

I filed for divorce.

Soon after that, my sister, Cindy, and her husband, Butch, introduced me to Philip. Their handsome friend became my drinking buddy, then confidant, then lover.

I got pregnant and put alcohol on hold, but only until our son was born. For the next seven years, I operated as a functioning alcoholic, working, raising my children and drinking. In 2004, I was cited with a DUI. I celebrated my release 20 days later — with a drink.

I drank to obliterate unknown memories. Sorrow consumed me as I consumed alcohol — and guilt over putting my kids through a separation, which forced them to choose whether to live with their mom or dad.

Like a kayak without an oar, I drank, adrift on the sea of oblivion.

❧❧❧

The cheery lights, sounds and bustle of Christmas suffocated me in 2006. Tami was pregnant with my first grandchild. Twice in 24 hours I had landed in the emergency room. My alcohol-soaked brain could hardly process the doctor's warning.

"Ma'am," he said, "your body is starting to show the consequences of alcohol abuse. Would you consider not drinking anymore?"

I nodded. "I'll stop at the New Year," I promised. Somehow I often found myself coming out of a blackout in a suicidal ideation mode. That scared me to think I would come out wanting to kill myself.

I popped open a beer on New Year's Day, thinking, *The day's not over yet.* My eyes squinted, trying to focus on the time: 2 p.m. I stared at the open can in my hands. *If I don't do this now, I never will.* With that, I returned to the kitchen, took every can of beer from the fridge and poured them down the sink.

God, I give my addiction to alcohol to you. Please help me stay sober.

God helped me keep my word, but embarrassment kept me from church. Philip continued drinking, but God's will, and mine, kept me from joining him.

The phone rang nine months later, while I was preparing to have wrist surgery. "Hello, Gert," Philip said on the other end. "I'm checking into detox ... right now."

Is it possible? My heart soared. *I need to find a church. I need to thank God that Philip is finally giving up drinking. I need to find the God I once knew.* Shame taunted me. *Where can I go?*

The next Sunday, my daughter picked me up for church.

"Where are we going?" she asked.

"I don't know ... you're the driver," I replied.

She drove me to the church where I'd taken her and her siblings as they grew up. Embarrassment propelled me to the back row and caused me to slip away after the service without introducing myself to the pastor. But I returned the next week and met Pastor Dana and his wife, Debbie.

The next weekend, I wandered, alone in my apartment, from room to room. Finally, I fell on my knees.

God has a plan for your life! The words pounded in my head. They pulsed through my being. Dad had often told me that as I grew up. I heard his words again.

God has a plan for your life, Paniga, he'd say. One day I asked him why he always said that to me.

He saved you from drowning, Dad explained, *at the age of 4 months. Our dogsled fell through the ice and into the water and got stuck. God sent Alfred Adams and his team along … just in time. He hitched his dogs to our sled and pulled it out.*

I wandered to the window, shaking. *You had drowned, Paniga. He performed CPR on you and brought you back to life … for a reason.*

"Okay, God," I said out loud. "At this moment, I submit my whole life to you — completely. I repent for all my sins. Please forgive me. I'm asking you to come into my heart and live within me. Help me. Please help me."

Philip came back sober. It didn't last.

"I can't take it," I cried to Pastor Dana and his wife, Debbie.

"Just keep praying," they encouraged. "God is able."

❧❧❧

OUT OF THE SHADOWS

"I just can't release my parents," I sobbed to Debbie. "They've been gone for years, but I can't let them go."

"Have you ever properly grieved for them?" Debbie asked.

I shook my head, mystified. *One does not discuss or think on bad times or sad times.* Our people's code of silence mocked me. For years, I used alcohol to dull the pain — every Father's and Mother's Day, every holiday, every birthday.

"I sense you feel abandoned," Debbie continued. "Let's pray about that."

As she prayed, I felt the monumental weight of grief lift off my shoulders. I felt I could finally straighten my shoulders and look life in the face.

Not long after that, Pastor Dana and Debbie introduced me to SOZO, a ministry of inner healing and deliverance. Through these prayers, I finally forgave all the perpetrators in my life. I felt taller, stronger and lighter. As tall and strong and light as an arrow — or a spear. And that is the meaning of my given name, Gertrude: Spear of Strength.

Mount Marathon towers over the town of Seward. I smile at its imposing stature. I have run my own marathon. My heart shouts with Paul's in 2 Timothy 4:7: "I have fought the good fight. I have completed the race. I have kept the faith."

Our town sits at the northern end of Resurrection Bay. God has saved and healed this mother of seven — and delivered me from a life of guilt, shame and unforgiveness.

PANIGA, MY DAUGHTER

I called on him, and he answered me. Already God has shown me great and mighty things that I had not known before (Jeremiah 33:3). I am ready to sail on *his* Resurrection Bay, facing whatever he has called me for — his cleansed and strengthened *Paniga of God.*

CONCLUSION

Each of these stories is unique in the details, but a common theme runs throughout all of them. It is the love of God that comes on the scene and changes everything for a person.

"This is how God showed his love among us: He sent his one and only Son into the world that we might live through him" (1 John 4:9).

"In him was life, and that life was the light of men. The light shines in the darkness" (John 1:4-5).

Jesus said, "I am the light of the world. Whoever follows me will never walk in darkness, but will have the light of life" (John 8:12).

For many of us, it is the easier road to close off our hearts and lock down our pain and mistakes. But this is not true life. True life is found in Christ, true freedom through coming to him, true hope and purpose by walking with him. "So if the Son sets you free, you will be free indeed" (John 8:36).

Jesus came to earth and died and rose again so that all mankind could be restored to a relationship with God. Because of him, all the shadows of sin will go, and we can find ourselves living under the shadow of Almighty God, safe and at peace.

When Jesus walked on the earth, he looked with great compassion on those who were broken and hurting — that is, all of us. Religion tries to fix the externals, but only

Christ can change the human heart. A set of rules will not change us; only Christ can.

He alone is able to bind up the brokenhearted, speak freedom to those in the captivity of unforgiveness for wrongs suffered and release from darkness those in prison. Think of the captives in war. They are there through no fault of their own. Those in heart captivity are there due to wounding by others and false beliefs. Jesus offers freedom from this captivity.

Prisoners are put in prison because of their own actions. We make ourselves prisoners when we sin, but when we come to Jesus broken and repentant, he opens the doors of our self-made prisons, offering us full forgiveness.

Jesus said, "When a man believes in me, he does not believe in me only, but in the one who sent me. When he looks at me, he sees the one who sent me. I have come into the world as a light, so that no one who believes in me should stay in darkness" (John 12:44-46).

If you are ready to walk out of the shadows and into the light of Christ to find salvation, deliverance from the bondages of unforgiveness, shame and guilt and the healing of mind, body and soul, he is waiting for you to come to him. Jesus wants to have a relationship with you, and he has done everything for this to be possible. You were created by God and for a relationship with God. Just talk to him, right now. If you still have questions, but feel a stirring in your heart, we would love to talk or pray with you.

Eagles Nest Christian Fellowship A/G
We meet Sunday mornings at10 a.m. at
437 2nd Avenue, Seward, AK 99664
(Blue church on corner of 2nd and Madison).

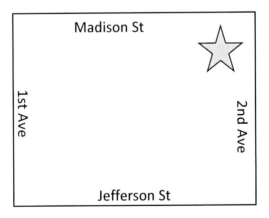

Please call us at 907.224.5635 for directions, or
contact us at www.eaglesnestofalaska.org.

For more information on reaching your city with
stories from your church, please contact
Good Catch Publishing at
www.goodcatchpublishing.com

GOOD CATCH
PUBLISHING

Did one of these stories touch you?
Did one of these real people move you to tears?
Tell us (and them) about it on our reader blog at
www.goodcatchpublishing.blogspot.com.